Career Planning

for College Students

A Comprehensive Guide to Essential Skills for Career Exploration and Development for Young Adults in the Digital Age

Isabella Wells

© **2024 by Isabella Wells**

All rights reserved. No part of this book may be reproduced or transmitted in any form or by any means, electronic or mechanical, including photocopying, recording, or by any information storage and retrieval system, without written permission from the author, except for the inclusion of brief quotations in a critical review.

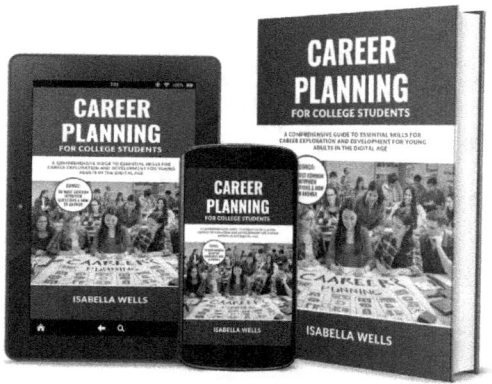

Table of Contents

Introduction — 7

Chapter One — 13

Discovering Your Unique Self — 13

    Exploring Personal Values, Interests, and Motivations — 13

    Assessing Personality Traits, Strengths, and Aptitudes — 16

    Developing a Growth Mindset for Personal and Professional Success — 19

Chapter Two — 25

Researching and Evaluating Career Pathways — 25

    Utilizing Career Exploration Tools and Resources — 25

    Understanding Job Outlooks, Growth Potential, and Industry Trends — 29

    Informational Interviewing and Job Shadowing Opportunities — 33

Chapter Three — 39
Choosing the Right Academic Path — 39

Selecting a College Major Aligned with Career Goals — 39

Understanding Graduate School and Professional Degree Options — 44

Creating a Four-Year Academic Plan and Mapping Prerequisites — 49

Chapter Four — 55
Cultivating Essential Skills for the Modern Workplace — 55

Developing Critical Thinking, Problem-Solving, and Adaptability — 55

Mastering Communication, Collaboration, and Emotional Intelligence — 60

Embracing Technological Literacy and Digital Fluency — 66

Chapter Five — 71
Building a Powerful Professional Brand — 71

Crafting Compelling Resumes, Cover Letters,

and Online Profiles 71

Leveraging Social Media and Networking Strategies 76

Developing a Personal Brand and Unique Value Proposition 80

Chapter Six **87**

Gaining Relevant Experience and Exposure 87

Securing Internships, Co-ops, and Apprenticeships 87

Exploring Student Organizations, Leadership Roles, and Volunteering 93

Understanding Industry-Specific Challenges and Nuances 99

Chapter Seven **107**

Mastering the Job Search and Recruitment Process **107**

Developing Effective Job Search Strategies and Resources 107

Acing Interviews and Negotiating Job Offers 112

    Understanding Employee Rights, Benefits, and Compensation Packages 118

Chapter Eight 125

Entrepreneurship and Self-Employment Considerations 125

    Evaluating the Entrepreneurial Mindset and Opportunities 125

    Developing a Business Plan, Securing Funding, and Legal Requirements 129

    Balancing Risks and Rewards of Self-Employment 134

Chapter Nine 141

Strategies for Career Advancement and Transitions 141

    Continuous Learning, Professional Development, and Upskilling 141

    Seeking Mentors, Sponsors, and Building Professional Networks 146

    Navigating Career Pivots, Transitions, and Alternative Pathways 152

Chapter Ten   **159**

Long-Term Career Planning and Financial Wellness   **159**

    Aligning Short-Term and Long-Term Career Goals   159

        Work-Life Balance, Stress Management, and Personal Fulfillment   163

    Financial Literacy, Retirement Planning, and Wealth-Building Strategies   168

Exclusive Bonus   **175**

    20 most Common Interview Questions & How to Answer Them   175

Introduction

Embarking on a college journey is a pivotal moment, filled with excitement, possibilities, and the promise of shaping one's future. Yet, amidst the thrill of newfound independence and intellectual exploration, a nagging question often lingers: "What's next?" The transition from classroom to career can be both exhilarating and daunting, leaving many students feeling uncertain about their path forward.

This is where "Career Planning for College Students" comes into play – a comprehensive guide that serves as a compass, illuminating the way towards a fulfilling and purposeful professional life. Within these pages lies a transformative adventure, a journey of self-discovery, and the keys to unlocking your true potential.

Imagine navigating the vast landscape of career options with confidence, armed with a deep understanding of your unique strengths, values, and aspirations. This book empowers you to shed the guise of uncertainty and embrace the authentic essence of who you are, aligning your passions with your professional pursuits.

As you delve into the chapters, you'll embark on a profound exploration of self, uncovering your unique personality, aptitudes, and motivations. With each turn of the page, you'll gain invaluable insights into the ever-evolving job market, equipping yourself with the knowledge to make informed decisions and seize emerging opportunities.

But this book is more than just a repository of information – it's a catalyst for personal growth and empowerment. Through engaging exercises and thought-provoking prompts, you'll cultivate essential skills that transcend the boundaries of any single career path. Critical thinking, adaptability, and emotional intelligence will become your allies, enabling you to thrive in the dynamic and ever-changing landscape of the modern workplace.

Imagine the confidence that comes with crafting a compelling personal brand, one that sets you apart and showcases your unique value proposition to potential employers. This book will guide you through the art of crafting captivating resumes, cover letters, and online profiles, ensuring that your authentic self shines through in every interaction.

Beyond the theoretical foundations, "Career Planning for College Students" offers a treasure trove of practical strategies and resources. From securing coveted internships and hands-on experiences to mastering the art of networking and acing interviews, you'll be armed with the tools to navigate the job search process with poise and confidence.

For those with an entrepreneurial spirit, this book unveils the exciting world of self-employment, equipping you with the knowledge to evaluate opportunities, develop business plans, and navigate the complexities of starting your own venture.

But the journey doesn't end with securing that dream job or launching a successful business. This book understands the ever-evolving nature of careers and the importance of continuous growth. You'll discover strategies for career advancement, pivoting into new roles, and maintaining a fulfilling work-life balance, ensuring that your professional aspirations remain aligned with your personal well-being.

Throughout this transformative experience, you'll be accompanied by the wisdom of seasoned professionals, mentors, and industry experts who have walked the path before you. Their insights, anecdotes, and real-world examples will illuminate the nuances of various career paths, providing a realistic and authentic perspective on the challenges and triumphs that lie ahead.

"Career Planning for College Students" is more than just a book – it's a testament to the boundless potential that lies within each and every one of us. It's a call to action, inviting you to embrace the exhilarating journey of self-discovery, and to chart a course that aligns with your deepest aspirations.

So, are you ready to embark on this enlightening adventure? To unlock the door to a world of possibilities and unleash the power of your true potential? Turn the page, and let the transformation begin.

Chapter One

Discovering Your Unique Self

Exploring Personal Values, Interests, and Motivations

Investigating your interests, values, and motives in depth is the first step in discovering your distinct identity. These fundamental aspects of your character and motivations have a significant role in determining your professional trajectory.

Core Principles:
Your values are the principles by which you live your life, make decisions, and find fulfillment. To choose a profession that suits your values, priorities, and beliefs, you must first know what they are. Some typical values to examine include

integrity, creativity, altruism, financial security, work-life balance, and intellectual stimulation.

Consider the choices you made and the feelings of happiness or dissatisfaction they evoked in the past to get a sense of your core values. To better understand your value system, it might be helpful to ask yourself questions like, "What do I value most in life?" and "What are my guiding principles?" It can also be helpful to ask close friends and family members for their perspectives.

Interests:
Your interests indicate the activities, themes, and subjects that engage your curiosity and excitement. Pursuing a career aligned with your passions can lead to improved job satisfaction, motivation, and general well-being. Interests might span from specific sectors like science, technology, or the arts to larger areas like problem-solving, working with people, or outdoor activities.

To define your interests, consider the hobbies, extracurricular activities, and academic courses that you find most enjoyable and intriguing. Reflect on the tasks or projects that energize you and make time fly by. Additionally, investigate online interest surveys or career exploration tools that can provide helpful insights based on your replies to numerous prompts and scenarios.

Motivations:
Motivations are the driving forces that urge you to take action and achieve specific goals. Understanding your motives might help you discover a career that not only corresponds with your values and interests but also delivers a sense of purpose and fulfillment.

Some typical motivations include a desire for creativity, intellectual challenge, leadership chances, making a positive influence, financial stability, or work-life balance. Reflect on the factors that continuously encourage you to put forth your best efforts and welcome new challenges.

It's also crucial to remember that values, interests, and motives can vary throughout time. Regularly reassessing and developing your understanding of these factors will help you stay true to your authentic self and make smart professional selections throughout your life path.

Assessing Personality Traits, Strengths, and Aptitudes

In addition to studying your values, interests, and motivations, it's vital to examine your personality traits, strengths, and aptitudes when discovering your unique self. These components can provide useful insights about the types of workplaces, roles, and career pathways that may be most fit for you.

Personality Traits:

Personality traits are the permanent patterns of thoughts, feelings, and behaviors that influence how you perceive and interact with the world around you. Understanding your personality features might help you select occupations that correspond with your natural tendencies and interests.

Some frequent personality traits to examine include extraversion/introversion, conscientiousness, openness to experience, agreeableness, and emotional stability. Various personality evaluations, such as the Myers-Briggs Type Indicator (MBTI) or the Big Five Personality Test, can reveal insights into your unique personality profile.

Strengths:

Strengths are the skills, abilities, and talents that you naturally succeed at and like utilizing. Identifying and exploiting your skills can lead to improved work happiness, productivity, and overall success.

Common talents can include analytical thinking, creativity, communication, teamwork, leadership, problem-solving, attention to detail, or emotional intelligence. Reflect on the tasks or activities that you consistently execute well and receive positive feedback on.

Additionally, seek input from individuals who know you well, such as family, friends, or mentors. They may offer significant perspectives on your distinct skills that you may not have discovered yourself.

Aptitudes:
Aptitudes are the intrinsic qualities or capacities that enable you to gain knowledge and skills more rapidly in specific areas. Recognizing your aptitudes might help you explore job paths that correspond with your inherent talents and potential.

Some frequent aptitudes include arithmetic reasoning, spatial awareness, verbal comprehension, mechanical reasoning, and memory retention. Aptitude exams or assessments can provide insights into your abilities and areas of potential brilliance.

It's crucial to highlight that while personality traits, talents, and aptitudes can impact your professional choices, they do not necessarily dictate your route. With dedication, effort, and a growth attitude, individuals can learn new skills and flourish in areas that may not have been first obvious.

Developing a Growth Mindset for Personal and Professional Success

Adopting a growth mindset is vital for personal and professional success, as it encourages individuals to embrace difficulties, learn from setbacks, and continuously expand their abilities. A growth mindset is the concept that intelligence, talents, and abilities are not fixed but can be cultivated through devotion, effort, and perseverance.

Embracing a Growth Mindset:
Developing a growth mindset includes altering your perspective away from the restrictive assumption that your talents and abilities are preset and unchangeable. Instead, it requires recognizing that with the correct mindset, techniques, and effort, you can continuously grow and improve.

Individuals with a growth mindset perceive setbacks as opportunities for learning and growth rather than insurmountable hurdles. They are more resilient in the face of setbacks, as they regard failures as transient and as opportunities to learn and better.

Cultivating a Growth Mindset:

Cultivating a growth mindset needs conscious work and a willingness to venture outside of your comfort zone. Here are some techniques to help cultivate this mindset:

1. **Reframe Your Perspective**: Consciously modify your internal conversation and self-talk to embrace a growth-oriented perspective. Instead of expressing "I'm not good at this," try reframing it as "I'm not good at this yet, but with practice, I can improve."

2. **Embrace Challenges**: Seek out challenging events and opportunities that stretch your abilities. Stepping outside of your comfort zone and addressing new difficulties fosters growth and learning.

3. **Learn from Setbacks**: Treat setbacks and failures as useful learning opportunities. Reflect on what went wrong, find areas for improvement, and adapt your strategy accordingly.

4. Seek Feedback: Actively seek feedback from others, such as mentors, teachers, or peers. Feedback can provide useful insights into your strengths, areas for improvement, and methods for progress.

5. applaud Effort and Progress: Recognize and applaud the effort you put into learning and growing, even if the rewards are not immediate. Acknowledge and appreciate the progress you made along the road.

Applying a Growth Mindset to Career Planning:

Developing a growth mindset is particularly important in the context of career planning and professional development. It empowers you to:

- Embrace ongoing learning and upskilling possibilities

- Adapt to shifting job market trends and industry expectations
- Explore new professional trajectories or pivots without fear of failure
- Seek out hard jobs and extend opportunities
- Persevere through setbacks and rejections during the job search process

By adopting a growth mindset, you equip yourself with the resilience, adaptability, and desire to negotiate the ever-changing professional landscape and unlock your full potential for personal and career progress.

Chapter Two

Researching and Evaluating Career Pathways

Utilizing Career Exploration Tools and Resources

In today's fast dynamic employment market, it's crucial to have access to the necessary tools and resources to efficiently explore and evaluate various career pathways. With a multitude of information available at our fingertips, accessing these tools can provide vital insights and direction along your career planning path.

Online Career Assessments:
Online career evaluations are useful tools that can help you uncover potential job options based on

your interests, values, personality traits, and abilities. These exams often entail answering a series of questions or prompts linked to your preferences, motivations, and abilities. Based on your responses, they develop individualized job recommendations linked to your unique profile.

Some prominent online career assessments include:

1. O*NET Interest Profiler: This free assessment from the U.S. Department of Labor helps locate occupations that fit your interests.

2. Myers-Briggs Type Indicator (MBTI): This widely renowned personality evaluation can provide insights into your preferred work styles and environments.

3. SkillScan: This tool examines your skills and aptitudes, recommending jobs that may be a suitable fit.

Career Exploration Websites:

In addition to tests, numerous websites are dedicated to helping individuals explore and research various career possibilities. These sites generally give thorough information on job descriptions, education requirements, income ranges, job outlook, and more.

Some significant career exploration websites include:

1. Occupational Outlook Handbook (OOH): This large resource from the U.S. Bureau of Labor Statistics offers thorough information on hundreds of vocations.

2. CareerOneStop: This website from the U.S. Department of Labor provides career exploration tools, job-seeking resources, and training information.

3. Glassdoor: In addition to job postings, Glassdoor offers insights into company culture, salary, and employee reviews.

Professional Associations and Industry Organizations:

Connecting with professional associations and industry organizations can be a helpful resource for acquiring insights into specific career pathways. These organizations often provide information on industry trends, career possibilities, and networking events.

Additionally, many associations offer career tools such as mentorship programs, job boards, and professional development opportunities. Joining these organizations can help you remain informed about the latest advancements in your subject of interest and connect with individuals who can offer assistance and advice.

University Career Centers:

As a college student, your university's career center should be one of your go-to options for career research and planning. Career counselors at these centers are trained specialists who can help you navigate the career planning process, from self-assessment to job search methods.

Career centers often offer several services, including:

1. One-on-one career coaching sessions
2. Resume and cover letter reviews
3. Mock interviews and interview preparation
4. Job and internship postings
5. Career fairs and employer networking events

Understanding Job Outlooks, Growth Potential, and Industry Trends

As you investigate various career choices, it's vital to grasp the job outlook, development potential, and industry trends associated with each profession. This knowledge can help you make informed decisions and better position yourself for long-term success in a dynamic employment market.

Job Outlook:
The job outlook refers to the predicted expansion or decline of employment possibilities within a given occupation or industry over a specific period. Understanding the job outlook can help you analyze the prospective demand for your intended career path and make strategic decisions about your education and training.

The U.S. Bureau of Labor Statistics (BLS) is a great site for acquiring job outlook statistics. The BLS releases detailed statistics on employment predictions, including:

1. Projected job growth rates for certain occupations
2. Industries having the highest job growth potential

3. Factors impacting job growth or reduction (e.g., technical improvements, industry trends, demographic shifts)

Growth Potential:

In addition to job outlook, it's crucial to assess the growth possibilities associated with different career pathways. Growth potential refers to the prospects for advancement, additional responsibility, and higher earning potential within a given field or organization.

Factors that can influence professional growth potential include:

1. Opportunities for professional development and continuous education
2. Availability of specialist certifications or higher degrees
3. Potential for leadership roles or management jobs

4. Emerging technology or industry developments that increase demand for new talents

By investigating development potential, you can select job options that offer long-term chances for personal and professional advancement.

Industry Trends:
Understanding industry trends is vital for staying ahead of the curve and making educated professional decisions. Industry trends can impact the job market, alter skill needs, and generate new possibilities or problems within a given profession.

Some major industrial trends to observe include:

1. Technological developments and digital transformations
2. Globalization and international trade dynamics
3. Changes in customer tastes or market demands

4. Regulatory or regulatory shifts impacting specific industries

5. Sustainability and environmental considerations

By remaining updated about industry trends, you may anticipate future skill requirements, uncover emerging possibilities, and position yourself as a valuable asset in your chosen sector.

Informational Interviewing and Job Shadowing Opportunities

While internet tools and industry studies can provide helpful insights, nothing can completely replace the firsthand knowledge and experiences gained through informative interviewing and work shadowing opportunities. These tactics offer a unique opportunity to engage with people in your desired area, obtain insider viewpoints, and make educated decisions regarding your career path.

Informational Interviewing:

An informational interview is a conversation with a professional in a field or sector that interests you. The major objective of these interviews is to gather information and insights, rather than to earn a job offer. Informational interviews can provide valuable perspectives on numerous elements of a certain career, including:

1. Day-to-day responsibilities and job duties
2. Educational and training requirements
3. Career growth and advancement opportunities
4. Work-life balance and organizational culture
5. Challenges and perks of the occupation

To perform an informational interview efficiently, follow these steps:

1. Identify professionals in your target sector or industry through your network, professional associations, or internet platforms like LinkedIn.

2. Reach out gently and suggest a brief meeting or phone chat to learn more about their work journey and experiences.

3. Prepare a list of insightful questions to ask during the interview.

4. Be courteous of the professional's time and avoid openly asking for a job or internship opportunity.

5. Follow up with a thank-you note and retain the connection for potential future networking possibilities.

Job Shadowing:

Job shadowing entails seeing a professional in their office setting for a designated length of time, generally a day or a few hours. This hands-on experience provides an up-close look at the everyday tasks, responsibilities, and work environment connected with a particular job.

Job shadowing can assist you:

1. Gain a realistic grasp of the job duties and company culture.
2. Observe the skills and knowledge required for the role.
3. Identify potential obstacles or components of the job that may not initially be visible.
4. Develop relationships and future mentorship possibilities within the business.

To gain job shadowing opportunities, start by reaching out to your personal and professional networks, including family, friends, professors, and alumni associations. Many corporations and organizations also offer official job shadowing programs or may fulfill requests on a case-by-case basis.

During the job shadowing experience, be an attentive observer and offer insightful questions when appropriate. Take notes on your observations and reflections, and be sure to convey your gratitude to the people or organization for giving this excellent learning opportunity.

Both informative interviewing and job shadowing can offer essential insights into potential career pathways, help you make educated decisions, and build your professional network. By actively engaging in these tactics, you can develop a greater awareness of the reality and complexities of many vocations, ultimately setting yourself up for long-term success and fulfillment in your chosen sector.

Chapter Three

Choosing the Right Academic Path

Selecting a College Major Aligned with Career Goals

Choosing the correct college major is a key decision that can dramatically affect your future job trajectory. While it's not necessary to have your complete professional path plotted out before selecting a major, connecting your academic program with your larger interests, values, and job objectives can set you up for success and fulfillment in the long term.

Understanding the Relationship Between Majors and Careers:

It's crucial to note that not all majors closely connect with specific jobs. Some majors, such as engineering, nursing, or accounting, have a more direct track to matching occupations. Others, like English, history, or psychology, can lead to a varied range of job opportunities across numerous industries.

Regardless of the major you pick, the information, skills, and critical thinking talents you gain will be great assets in the employment market. Employers frequently prefer well-rounded workers with good communication, problem-solving, and analytical talents, in addition to specific technical expertise.

Exploring Major Options:
As you research potential majors, consider the following factors:

1. Your interests and passions: Choose a major that aligns with subjects, issues, or sectors that genuinely excite and motivate you.

2. Your skills and aptitudes: Assess your inherent abilities and select a major that allows you to utilize and further develop your strengths.

3. job opportunities: Research the prospective job routes connected with each major and examine their growth prospects, earning potential, and connection with your goals.

4. Experiential learning options: Look for majors that offer possibilities for internships, co-ops, research projects, or other hands-on experiences to boost your education and career readiness.

Utilize resources such as your university's academic advising center, career services office, and department websites to obtain information on major requirements, course options, and potential career routes.

Strategies for Aligning Your Major with Career Goals:

If you have a specific career in mind, explore the following strategies:

1. Seek help from professionals in your selected field to understand the school requirements and recommended majors.
2. Research job advertisements and descriptions to determine the qualifications and talents employers are seeking.
3. Explore interdisciplinary or customizable major options that allow you to combine complementary fields of study.
4. Consider pursuing a minor, double major, or certificate program to boost your skills and marketability in your intended professional field.

If you're undecided or have broad interests, consider the following:

1. Choose a major that provides a strong foundation in transferable abilities (e.g., critical thinking,

communication, problem-solving) relevant to numerous careers.

2. Explore liberal arts or general studies programs that allow you to taste numerous subjects before committing to a specific degree.

3. Take advantage of career evaluations, informational interviews, and job shadowing opportunities to obtain insights into various career routes.

4. Remain open to altering your major as your interests and ambitions grow throughout your college experience.

Remember, your degree is not a lifelong commitment, and many successful individuals have followed occupations outside of their original field of study. The idea is to choose a major that matches your current interests and aspirations while being flexible and open to new chances that may occur throughout your academic and career experience.

Understanding Graduate School and Professional Degree Options

For many employment routes, getting an advanced degree or professional certification can be a significant investment in your future. Graduate school and professional degree programs offer specialized instruction, in-depth information, and a greater reputation within your chosen area. Understanding the numerous options available will help you make informed decisions about furthering your education and attaining your long-term job goals.

Master's Degrees:
A master's degree is a graduate-level academic program that normally takes one to two years to complete after receiving a bachelor's degree. Master's degrees are meant to provide advanced knowledge and specific skills in a particular area or career.

Some common forms of master's degrees include:

1. **Master of Arts (M.A.) or Master of Science (M.S.):** These degrees are widely pursued in sectors such as education, humanities, social sciences, and some scientific disciplines.

2. **Master of Business Administration (MBA):** An MBA is a common choice for individuals seeking leadership and management responsibilities in numerous industries.

3. **Master of Engineering (M.Eng.) or Master of Science in Engineering (M.S.E.):** These degrees prepare students for advanced technical and engineering positions.

4. **Master of Public Health (MPH) or Master of Social Work (MSW):** These programs train professionals for positions in healthcare, social services, and community organizations.

Doctoral Degrees:

Doctoral degrees, such as the Doctor of Philosophy (Ph.D.) or professional doctorates (e.g., Ed.D., D.B.A.), signify the greatest level of academic achievement. These programs often entail considerable study, coursework, and a dissertation or doctoral thesis.

Pursuing a Ph.D. degree may be advantageous for persons interested in academics, research, or leadership roles in their respective industries. However, it's necessary to carefully assess the time, financial commitment, and professional ambitions connected with a PhD degree.

Professional Degrees:
In addition to academic graduate programs, many professions demand specific professional degrees or certificates. These programs are designed to give the specific information and abilities necessary for entry and advancement within a particular field.

Some examples of professional degrees include:

1. Medicine (M.D. or D.O.)
2. Law (J.D.)
3. Dentistry (D.D.S. or D.M.D.)
4. Pharmacy (Pharm.D.)
5. Veterinary Medicine (D.V.M.)
6. Architecture (M.Arch.)

Professional degree programs sometimes have special admissions requirements, such as specified preparatory courses, standardized assessments, and practical experience.

Factors to Consider:

When investigating graduate school and professional degree alternatives, consider the following factors:

1. Career goals and development opportunities: Evaluate how the degree matches your intended

career path and opportunity for professional progress.

2. Program reputation and accreditation: Research the quality and reputation of the programs you're considering, as well as their accreditation status.

3. Cost and funding opportunities: Graduate and professional programs can be expensive, so seek funding sources such as scholarships, assistantships, and employer tuition aid.

4. Program format and flexibility: Determine if you want a regular on-campus program, online choices, or a combination of both.

5. Prerequisites and admissions requirements: Ensure you meet the relevant prerequisites and understand the application procedure and deadlines.

Additionally, consider seeking guidance from specialists in your desired industry, as well as career counselors and academic advisors, to help you navigate the decision-making process.

Creating a Four-Year Academic Plan and Mapping Prerequisites

Developing a thorough four-year academic plan is vital for remaining on track toward your academic and career goals. By planning out your course requirements, prerequisites, and prospective experiential learning opportunities, you can ensure a seamless progression through your college adventure and position yourself for success after graduation.

Importance of Academic Planning:
Creating an academic plan gives various benefits:

1. Efficient degree completion: Proper preparation lets you accomplish all degree requirements within the desired timeframe, avoiding delays or additional study.

2. Prerequisite management: Many courses have specified prerequisites that must be completed beforehand. Planning ensures you achieve these requirements in the optimal sequence.

3. Opportunity exploration: An academic plan allows you to carefully include internships, research projects, study abroad programs, or other beneficial experiences into your timetable.

4. Financial planning: By sketching out your academic journey, you may better anticipate tuition costs and plan for prospective scholarship or financial aid needs.

5. Stress reduction: Having a clear roadmap can lessen the worry and ambiguity that sometimes accompany academic decision-making.

Steps for Creating an Academic Plan:

1. Review degree requirements: Thoroughly comprehend the precise course requirements, credit hours, and any additional expectations (e.g., capstone projects, internships) for your chosen major and degree program.

2. Identify prerequisites: Carefully read course descriptions and prerequisites to establish the right sequence of classes. Some courses may have numerous prerequisites that need to be completed in a specific order.

3. Incorporate general education requirements: In addition to major-specific courses, most degree programs require a set of general education courses in disciplines including humanities, social sciences, and natural sciences.

4. Consider experiential learning opportunities: Explore choices for internships, co-ops, study abroad programs, or undergraduate research projects that can increase your academic and professional advancement.

5. Map out your schedule: Using your institution's course catalog and academic advising materials, build a rough semester-by-semester plan that encompasses all necessary courses, prerequisites, and prospective experiential learning opportunities.

6. Remain flexible: While a well-crafted academic plan is vital, be prepared to make adjustments when your interests, ambitions, or circumstances evolve throughout your college adventure.

Utilizing Academic Advising Resources:
Your institution's academic advising office is a helpful resource for designing and modifying your academic plan. Academic advisors can guide degree requirements, course options, and techniques for keeping on track. They can also help you negotiate any obstacles or adjustments that may happen along the road.

Additionally, many colleges offer degree audit tools or online academic planning systems that allow you to track your progress, explore course possibilities, and ensure you're completing all requirements.

Balancing Academic and Personal Commitments:

When constructing your academic plan, it's crucial to consider not only your schoolwork but also any additional commitments or tasks you may have. This could be a part-time job, extracurricular activities, family duties, or personal hobbies.

Effective time management and prioritization skills will be vital in balancing these diverse parts of your life. Be realistic in your plans and allow for flexibility to handle unexpected conditions or opportunities that may arise.

By investing time and effort into constructing a thorough four-year academic plan, you can navigate your college experience with confidence and clarity. This proactive strategy will assist you stay on track toward your academic and career goals while maximizing the value of your college education.

54

Chapter Four

Cultivating Essential Skills for the Modern Workplace

Developing Critical Thinking, Problem-Solving, and Adaptability

In today's quickly developing corporate scene, the capacity to think critically, solve difficult problems, and adapt to change is important for success in the modern workplace. These abilities are highly recognized by employers across industries and can help you overcome the problems and seize the opportunities that arise throughout your career.

Critical Thinking:
Critical thinking is the ability to assess information objectively, consider many perspectives, and make

educated conclusions based on logical reasoning and facts. It involves:

1. Questioning assumptions and challenging conventional wisdom
2. Evaluating the credibility and dependability of sources
3. Identifying patterns, relationships, and underlying issues
4. Drawing well-reasoned findings and generating clear arguments

Developing critical thinking abilities is vital for efficiently navigating complicated situations, making solid judgments, and generating innovation within an organization.

Problem-Solving:
Successful problem-solving is the capacity to identify and characterize difficulties, produce and assess alternative solutions, and implement

successful ways to overcome hurdles. This method normally involves:

1. Clearly describing the problem and acquiring essential facts
2. Generating many solutions through creative thought and brainstorming
3. Analyzing the advantages and cons of each solution and selecting the most acceptable strategy
4. Developing a plan for implementation and monitoring progress
5. Adjusting techniques as appropriate and learning from the experience

Strong problem-solving abilities are invaluable in every field, as they help you tackle difficulties head-on, create inventive solutions, and promote continual growth within a company.

Adaptability:

In the modern workplace, change is constant, and the capacity to adapt to new situations, technology, and methods of working is vital for long-term success. Adaptability involves:

1. Embracing a growth attitude and being open to learning and development
2. Remaining flexible and responding to altering priorities and expectations
3. Navigating ambiguity and uncertainty with resilience
4. Continuously upskilling and obtaining new information and competencies
5. Seeking for and embracing chances for personal and professional growth

Cultivating adaptability may help you survive in dynamic circumstances, respond effectively to emerging industry trends, and position yourself as a valued asset in any workplace.

Developing Critical Thinking, Problem-Solving, and Adaptability:

Cultivating these fundamental talents involves a combination of formal education, practical experience, and conscious effort. Here are some techniques to help you build and perfect these abilities:

1. Engage in active learning activities, such as case studies, simulations, or project-based assignments, that challenge you to use critical thinking and problem-solving abilities in real-world circumstances.
2. Seek out other ideas and engage in constructive debates or discussions to widen your awareness and question your assumptions.
3. Regularly practice analytical and creative thinking exercises, such as puzzles, brain teasers, or design challenges, to strengthen your problem-solving talents.
4. Embrace opportunities for ongoing learning, such as taking additional classes, attending workshops, or engaging in professional development programs.

5. Step outside your comfort zone and expose yourself to new experiences, cultures, or ways of thinking to develop adaptability and an open attitude.

6. Seek feedback and mentorship from experienced professionals to gain insights and guidance on developing these important abilities.

By actively practicing critical thinking, problem-solving, and adaptability, you will empower yourself with the crucial tools to manage the challenges of the modern workplace, create innovation, and position yourself for long-term career success.

Mastering Communication, Collaboration, and Emotional Intelligence

Effective communication, strong teamwork skills, and emotional intelligence are basic characteristics for success in the modern workplace. These interpersonal qualities not only boost productivity and teamwork but also contribute to developing a positive and inclusive work atmosphere.

Communication:
Effective communication involves the capacity to transmit ideas, information, and messages effectively and simply, both in written and conversational forms. Strong communication abilities encompass:

1. Active listening and comprehension
2. Clear and articulate expression
3. Adapting communication approaches to varied populations
4. Utilizing suitable tone, body language, and nonverbal clues
5. Providing constructive comments and receiving input with an open mentality

Mastering communication skills is vital for building solid professional connections, influencing and persuading people, and ensuring that information is accurately received and acted upon.

Collaboration:

In today's team-oriented workplaces, the ability to interact effectively is vital. Successful teamwork involves:

1. Understanding and valuing diverse ideas and backgrounds
2. Actively contributing to group debates and decision-making processes
3. Resolving problems and finding common ground through compromise and negotiation
4. Sharing knowledge and resources to achieve joint goals
5. Fostering a positive and inclusive team environment

Strong collaboration abilities help teams to exploit diverse strengths, produce innovative ideas, and achieve collective achievement productively and harmoniously.

Emotional Intelligence:

Emotional intelligence (EQ) is the ability to perceive, analyze, and control one's own emotions, as well as the emotions of others. High emotional intelligence is described by:

1. Self-awareness and self-regulation
2. Empathy and understanding others' viewpoints
3. Effective stress management and resilience
4. Fostering strong relationships and societal awareness
5. Motivating and motivating others via emotional intelligence

Individuals with significant emotional intelligence are more suited to handle interpersonal dynamics, build trust and rapport, and create a happy and productive work environment.

Developing Communication, Collaboration, and Emotional Intelligence:
Cultivating these interpersonal abilities needs a combination of formal training, practical experience, and conscious effort. Here are some techniques to help you build and perfect these abilities:

1. Seek out opportunities to develop and refine your communication skills, such as public speaking, presentations, or writing activities.
2. Engage in team-based projects, group assignments, or extracurricular activities that demand collaboration and teamwork.
3. Participate in workshops, seminars, or courses focusing on increasing interpersonal skills, conflict resolution, and emotional intelligence.
4. Seek input from peers, mentors, or supervisors about your communication, teamwork, and

emotional intelligence strengths and areas for improvement.

5. Develop self-awareness by reflecting on your emotions, behaviors, and relationships with others, and make conscious efforts to change.

6. Practice active listening, empathy, and emotional regulation in both personal and professional settings.

7. Engage in role-playing exercises or simulations that allow you to practice communication, collaboration, and emotional intelligence in a safe and controlled environment.

By actively practicing these interpersonal skills, you will not only boost your effectiveness in the workplace but also contribute to building a positive and productive environment that fosters collaboration, trust, and mutual understanding.

Embracing Technological Literacy and Digital Fluency

In the digital age, technology literacy and digital fluency have become important abilities for success in the modern job. As technology continues to grow rapidly, the ability to successfully navigate and exploit digital tools and platforms is vital for boosting productivity, collaboration, and innovation across numerous industries and professions.

Technological Literacy:
Technological literacy refers to the ability to understand, use, and adapt to developing technology. It encompasses:

1. Proficiency in using common software applications, digital tools, and gadgets
2. Understanding the basic ideas and capabilities of diverse technologies

3. Ability to learn and adapt to new technologies as they appear

4. Critical appraisal of the advantages, limitations, and ethical implications of technology

5. Integrating technology efficiently into workflows and decision-making processes

Developing technological literacy helps individuals to work efficiently, stay relevant, and use the power of technology to create innovation and productivity in their particular industries.

Digital Fluency:

Digital fluency is the capacity to effectively communicate, cooperate, and create using digital tools and platforms. It involves:

1. Proficiency in using digital communication channels (e.g., email, instant messaging, video conferencing)

2. Leveraging online collaboration platforms and project management tools

3. Creating and sharing digital content (e.g., documents, presentations, multimedia)

4. Engaging with social media and online communities for networking and knowledge sharing

5. Utilizing digital tools for data analysis, visualization, and decision-making

Digital fluency helps individuals to efficiently navigate the digital landscape, work smoothly with remote teams, and employ digital tools to boost productivity and innovation.

Cultivating Technological Literacy and Digital Fluency:

Developing these talents needs a combination of formal education, hands-on experience, and a commitment to ongoing learning. Here are some techniques to help you cultivate technical literacy and digital fluency:

1. Regularly study and experiment with new technologies, software apps, and digital tools to increase your knowledge and talents.

2. Participate in workshops, online tutorials, or specialized training programs given by your institution, workplace, or industry groups.

3. Seek out opportunities to work on projects or assignments that demand the use of digital tools, allowing you to use your abilities in real contexts.

4. Stay informed about upcoming technology and trends by following industry journals, blogs, and thought leaders in your profession.

5. Engage in online groups, forums, or professional networks to learn from peers and professionals, share expertise, and collaborate on digital projects.

6. Develop a growth mentality and embrace a willingness to learn and adapt to new technologies as they emerge.

7. Seek comments and help from mentors or experienced experts on exploiting technology efficiently in your sector.

In addition to improving technical expertise, it's necessary to nurture critical thinking abilities and digital ethics to ensure responsible and ethical use of technology in the workplace. This involves comprehending privacy and data security considerations, as well as the potential ramifications and biases inherent in digital tools and algorithms.

By adopting technological literacy and digital fluency, you will position yourself as a valued asset in the modern workplace, armed with the abilities to drive innovation, collaborate successfully, and utilize the power of technology to achieve success in your chosen career path.

Chapter Five

Building a Powerful Professional Brand

Crafting Compelling Resumes, Cover Letters, and Online Profiles

In today's competitive job market, creating a strong personal brand is vital for sticking out and placing yourself as a top applicant. Your CV, cover letter, and online profiles serve as effective tools to present your unique abilities, experiences, and value proposition to potential employers. Crafting engaging materials that properly explain your qualifications and fit for a career can dramatically boost your chances of landing interviews and employment offers.

Resumes:

Your resume is frequently the first impression a potential employer will have of you, so it's vital to ensure it is well-structured, easy to read and showcases your most relevant qualifications. Key elements of a good résumé include:

1. Clear and concise formatting: Use a clean layout with suitable spacing, consistent formatting, and easy-to-scan parts.
2. Targeted objective or summary statement: Craft a compelling introduction statement that encapsulates your career aspirations and showcases your unique value offer.
3. Quantifiable achievements: Instead of merely describing job activities, emphasize your accomplishments and contributions using concrete, quantitative examples.
4. Relevant keywords: Incorporate industry-specific keywords and phrases that fit with the job requirements to ensure your resume is optimized for applicant tracking systems (ATS).

5. **Customization**: Tailor your CV to each single employment opportunity, highlighting the most relevant abilities and experiences for that particular post.

Cover Letters:

While sometimes ignored, a well-crafted cover letter may be a strong tool for showing your written communication abilities, excitement, and grasp of the profession and firm. Effective cover letters should:

1. Demonstrate your knowledge of the organization and role: Research the firm and position to highlight how your qualifications and experiences connect with their specific demands.

2. Tell a captivating story: Use the cover letter to express your unique background, motivations, and the value you can bring to the organization.

3. Highlight relevant accomplishments: Provide particular examples of achievements or initiatives that closely connect to the job criteria.

4. Express your enthusiasm and fit: Communicate your genuine interest in the role and firm, and explain why you are a great match for the position.

5. Follow appropriate formatting and etiquette: Ensure your cover letter is formatted professionally, free of typos, and complies with any submission rules offered by the employer.

Online Profiles:

In the digital age, your online presence is an extension of your professional identity. Platforms like LinkedIn, personal websites, and online portfolios offer possibilities to present your abilities, experiences, and accomplishments to a wider audience, including potential employers, industry professionals, and networking contacts.

1. **LinkedIn**: Optimize your LinkedIn profile by producing an engaging headline, crafting a well-written summary, and highlighting your relevant talents, experiences, and endorsements.

2. Personal Website or Online Portfolio: Consider developing a personal website or online portfolio to present your work samples, projects, and accomplishments in a visually appealing and interactive style.

3. Consistent Branding: Ensure that your online profiles and materials (resume, cover letter, website) have a consistent tone, language, and visual branding to promote your professional identity.

4. Online Presence Management: Regularly monitor and edit your online presence, including social media sites, to ensure a favorable and professional picture is portrayed.

By developing appealing resumes, cover letters, and web profiles, you can successfully explain your unique value proposition, emphasize your qualifications and achievements, and boost your exposure to potential employers and industry leaders.

Leveraging Social Media and Networking Strategies

In today's interconnected world, social media and networking methods have become vital components of developing a great professional brand. These platforms offer significant opportunities to engage with industry leaders, remain informed about current trends and developments, and exhibit your knowledge and accomplishments.

Social Media Strategies:
Social media platforms provide a significant outlet for professional networking, knowledge sharing, and personal branding. Here are some techniques to exploit social media effectively:

1. **LinkedIn**: Optimize your LinkedIn profile to display your professional successes, talents, and experiences. Engage with relevant industry groups,

share valuable content, and network with professionals in your sector.

2. **Twitter**: Utilize Twitter to follow industry leaders, participate in important conversations, contribute valuable content, and promote yourself as a thought leader in your area of expertise.

3. **Professional Blogs or Online Publications**: Consider writing articles or guest posts to industry-specific blogs or online publications to demonstrate your knowledge and establish yourself as a subject matter expert.

4. **Online Communities and Forums**: Engage with relevant online communities and forums about your field or interests. Contribute to debates, offer advice, and create relationships with like-minded experts.

5. **Content Creation and Curation**: Share valuable content, such as blog articles, whitepapers,

or industry updates, that highlights your knowledge and delivers value to your network.

Networking Strategies:
Effective networking is vital for creating relationships, identifying career prospects, and growing your professional contacts. Here are some techniques to increase your networking efforts:

1. **Attend Industry Events and Conferences**: Participate in local, regional, or national industry events, conferences, and trade exhibitions to meet with people in your field, learn about emerging trends, and grow your network.

2. **Join Professional Associations**: Get engaged with professional associations or organizations about your industry or area of interest. Attend meetings, volunteer for committees, and take advantage of networking opportunities.

3. **Informational Interviews**: Conduct informational interviews with professionals in your target sector or business to gain insights, and guidance, and maybe unearth career prospects or connections.

4. **Leverage Your Network**: Tap into your existing network of connections, including classmates, instructors, colleagues, and friends, to uncover prospective networking opportunities or introductions within your preferred field.

5. **Follow-Up and Nurture Connections**: After building new connections, follow up immediately, exchange contact information, and nurture those relationships by delivering value, sharing updates, or suggesting chances for collaboration.

Remember, networking is a two-way street. Approach it with an attitude of genuinely establishing relationships and delivering value to others, rather than merely seeking selfish advantage. Effective networking takes active listening, sincerity, and a willingness to help people in your professional group.

By employing social media and networking methods successfully, you may establish a powerful professional brand, grow your industry connections, and boost your exposure to possible employers and opportunities.

Developing a Personal Brand and Unique Value Proposition

In today's competitive employment market, having a strong personal brand and a clearly defined distinctive value proposition can set you apart from other candidates and position you for long-term career success. Your personal brand is the unique combination of talents, experiences, values, and traits that define who you are professionally, while your unique value proposition communicates the precise value you can bring to an employer or organization.

Defining Your Personal Brand:

Your personal brand should be an honest expression of your professional identity, values, and objectives. To define your personal brand, consider the following elements:

1. **basic Values and Beliefs**: Identify the concepts, ethical standards, and basic beliefs that influence your professional decisions and activities.

2. **Strengths and Expertise**: Assess your unique abilities, knowledge, and areas of expertise that differentiate you from others in your sector.

3. **Personality Traits and Communication Style**: Recognize how your personality traits, communication style, and interpersonal skills impact your professional interactions and relationships.

4. **Passions and Interests**: Identify the topics, hobbies, or causes that genuinely thrill and motivate you both personally and professionally.

5. **Career Goals and Aspirations**: Clearly identify your long-term career goals and the effect you expect to create in your chosen field or industry.

Once you have a firm knowledge of these factors, develop a succinct and engaging personal brand statement that captures the core of who you are as a professional and what you have to offer.

Developing Your Unique Value Proposition: Your unique value proposition (UVP) is a concise and persuasive statement that articulates the specific value you can deliver to an employer or organization. A well-defined UVP should:

1. **Highlight Your Differentiators**: Identify the distinctive talents, experiences, or qualities that set you apart from other candidates in your field.

2. Address Business Needs: Demonstrate how your unique qualities align with the specific objectives, issues, or goals of the business or organization.

3. Quantify Your Impact: Use actual examples, metrics, or successes to illustrate the quantifiable value you can bring.

4. Be Concise and Memorable: Craft a clear and brief message that is easy to comprehend and remember, expressing the essence of what makes you important.

Effectively communicating your unique value proposition is critical during job interviews, networking events, and throughout your job search and career growth. It helps potential employers understand how you can contribute to their organization and why they should hire or promote you above other candidates.

Aligning Personal Brand and Career Goals:

Your personal brand and distinctive value proposition should be closely aligned with your long-term career goals and aspirations. Consider the following measures to assure consistency and authenticity:

1. Identify Your job route: Clearly define the job route or industry you desire to follow, and tailor your personal brand and UVP to resonate with that specific field or sector.

2. Continuous Professional Development: Regularly examine and update your skills, knowledge, and expertise to ensure your personal brand remains current and aligned with your developing career goals.

3. Seek input: Solicit input from mentors, colleagues, or trusted advisers to acquire insights into how your personal brand is perceived and find areas for growth or refinement.

4. Consistently reflect Your Brand: Ensure that your CV, cover letters, online profiles, and professional interactions consistently reflect your personal brand and distinctive value proposition.

By building a strong personal brand and clearly communicating your unique value proposition, you can effectively position yourself as a standout candidate, communicate your value to potential employers, and boost your prospects of attaining long-term career success and fulfillment.

Chapter Six

Gaining Relevant Experience and Exposure

Securing Internships, Co-ops, and Apprenticeships

Internships, co-ops, and apprenticeships are important opportunities for college students to obtain practical, hands-on experience in their selected profession, develop essential skills, and explore potential career options. These experiences not only boost your résumé and marketability but also give you a competitive edge when transferring into the workforce after graduation.

Internships:

Internships are often short-term, temporary engagements that provide students the opportunity to work in a professional setting and receive practical experience relating to their field of study. Internships can be paid or unpaid and may be available during the school year or during the summer.

Benefits of internships include:

1. Practical skill development: Apply classroom information to real-world circumstances and build critical professional abilities such as problem-solving, communication, and teamwork.
2. business exposure: Gain insights into the day-to-day operations, culture, and expectations of a given business or company.
3. Networking opportunities: Connect with professionals in your target field, create contacts, and maybe secure references or future employment leads.

4. Career exploration: Explore numerous career pathways and assess if a particular function or industry corresponds with your interests and ambitions.

5. Resume enhancement: Demonstrate relevant experience and accomplishments to potential employers, boosting your competitiveness in the employment market.

Co-ops (Cooperative Education):

Co-ops, or cooperative education programs, are planned work experiences that mix classroom learning with numerous periods of full-time, paid employment in a professional context. Co-ops often alternate between academic semesters and work terms, allowing students to get considerable practical experience before graduating.

Benefits of co-ops include:

1. Longer-term industry immersion: Gain in-depth exposure to a company or industry during many

work terms, generally lasting several months or a year.

2. Skill development and application: Apply and polish your skills in a real-world situation, boosting your competency and job preparedness.

3. Financial compensation: Co-ops give paid work experience, helping to balance college fees and establish financial independence.

4. Potential for full-time employment: Many co-op firms use these programs as a recruitment funnel, offering full-time work to top-performing students following graduation.

Apprenticeships:

Apprenticeships are structured training programs that combine on-the-job training with classroom education, generally in skilled crafts or technical disciplines. Apprentices work under the leadership of experienced experts, learning through hands-on practice and formal study.

Benefits of apprenticeships include:

1. Earn as you learn: Apprentices receive paid on-the-job training and typically have their classroom instruction fees reimbursed by their employer or sponsor.

2. Mentorship and guidance: Work closely with experienced professionals who provide direction, training, and support throughout the apprenticeship program.

3. Industry-recognized credentials: Upon completion, apprentices gain industry-recognized certifications or licenses, enhancing their employability and earning potential.

4. Direct path to work: Many apprenticeships lead to full-time employment possibilities with the sponsoring firm or organization.

Securing Internships, Co-ops, and Apprenticeships:

To boost your chances of gaining these valuable experiences, explore the following strategies:

1. Start early: Begin your search well in advance, as many opportunities have competitive application processes and deadlines.

2. Utilize campus resources: Work closely with your university's career services office, visit career fairs, and leverage alumni networks to uncover potential opportunities.

3. Tailor your application materials: Customize your CV, cover letter, and other application materials to highlight your relevant abilities, experiences, and passion for the unique opportunity.

4. Network and create connections: Attend industry events, perform informational interviews, and interact with individuals in your target field to hear about potential positions.

5. Prepare for interviews: Research the organization, practice answering common interview questions, and be prepared to express your goals, talents, and interest in the position.

By securing internships, co-ops, or apprenticeships during your college years, you will not only gain invaluable practical experience but also enhance your marketability, develop essential professional skills, and explore potential career paths, setting yourself up for long-term success in your chosen field.

Exploring Student Organizations, Leadership Roles, and Volunteering

Engaging in student organizations, taking on leadership responsibilities, and participating in volunteering activities can give invaluable experiences that complement your academic goals and promote your personal and professional growth. These activities give opportunities to build vital skills, explore your interests, and make meaningful contributions to your school and local community.

Student Organizations:

Student organizations are structured groups or clubs that bring together individuals with shared interests, aims, or concerns. Participating in these groups can bring numerous benefits, including:

1. **Developing leadership and teamwork skills**: Many student groups provide opportunities to take on leadership roles, such as serving on an executive board or leading a committee, building skills in project management, delegation, and collaboration.

2. **Exploring interests and passions**: With a varied selection of organizations available, from academic clubs to cultural groups to leisure activities, you can explore and cultivate your personal and professional interests.

3. **Networking and creating connections**: Student organizations give a platform to engage with like-minded individuals, build ties with peers

and instructors, and grow your professional network.

4. Event planning and execution: Organizing and executing events, conferences, or fundraisers through student organizations can help you build vital skills in project management, budgeting, marketing, and event coordination.

5. Personal and professional growth: By venturing outside your comfort zone and taking on new tasks within student groups, you can nurture personal growth, develop resilience, and obtain useful experiences that contribute to your overall professional development.

Leadership Roles:

Assuming leadership roles within student clubs, academic programs, or campus initiatives can give tremendous possibilities for personal and professional growth. These responsibilities not only demonstrate your passion and initiative but also help you to acquire critical abilities such as:

1. Strategic planning and vision: As a leader, you will have the chance to define goals, formulate plans, and implement methods to accomplish desired outcomes.

2. Communication and public speaking: Leading meetings, presenting projects, and promoting your organization will strengthen your communication and public speaking talents.

3. Conflict resolution and problem-solving: Navigating problems, resolving disagreements, and finding creative solutions are key components of leadership responsibilities.

4. Mentorship and delegation: Effective leaders learn to delegate responsibilities, provide direction and support to team members, and promote a healthy and productive team atmosphere.

5. Time management and prioritization: Balancing many obligations and priorities is a critical ability that leadership roles can help you acquire.

Volunteering:

Volunteering is a fantastic way to obtain practical experience, develop essential skills, and have a good influence on your community. Volunteering possibilities might range from short-term activities or projects to regular commitments with local groups or non-profits. The benefits of volunteering include:

1. **Hands-on experience**: Volunteering allows you to use your knowledge and abilities in real-world settings, obtaining practical experience that can strengthen your résumé and employment prospects.

2. **Developing empathy and cultural awareness**: Working with diverse populations and communities can foster empathy, cultural awareness, and a deeper knowledge of societal concerns.

3. **Networking and creating connections**: Volunteering can introduce you to professionals, community leaders, and possible mentors who share your interests and passions.

4. Exploring prospective career pathways: By volunteering in different organizations or industries, you can obtain insights into numerous career options and identify which areas correspond best with your interests and aspirations.

5. own growth and fulfillment: Volunteering may be a pleasant and fulfilling activity that adds to your growth, helps you build a sense of purpose, and makes a positive impact on the lives of others.

To maximize the benefits of student groups, leadership roles, and volunteering, it's vital to approach these experiences with devotion, professionalism, and a commitment to continual learning and improvement. Reflect on the skills and knowledge obtained, seek feedback from mentors or advisors, and be deliberate about leveraging these experiences to promote your personal and professional development.

Understanding Industry-Specific Challenges and Nuances

While acquiring practical experience through internships, co-ops, student organizations, and volunteering is vital, it's also crucial to build an awareness of the industry-specific issues and intricacies that exist in your intended area. Every industry has its unique mix of dynamics, trends, and considerations that might affect your career path and the abilities required for success.

Industry Trends and Disruptions:
Staying educated about industry trends and potential disruptions is vital for steering your career path effectively. Some crucial areas to monitor include:

1. **Technological advancements**: Rapidly emerging technology can dramatically impact numerous industries, resulting in shifts in

employment responsibilities, skill requirements, and labor needs. For example, the rise of artificial intelligence, automation, and big data analytics has altered areas like manufacturing, banking, and healthcare.

2. Regulatory and policy changes: Changes in government laws, policies, or industry standards can have far-reaching effects on some sectors. For instance, environmental restrictions may harm the energy or manufacturing businesses, while data privacy laws might affect the tech and digital marketing sectors.

3. Shifting customer demands: Evolving consumer preferences and behaviors can drive changes within industries, requiring organizations to modify their products, services, and business structures. The development of e-commerce, for example, has disrupted traditional retail sectors, while the growing desire for sustainable and eco-friendly products has influenced numerous manufacturing and consumer goods businesses.

4. Global economic and market conditions: Economic issues such as recessions, trade regulations, and market swings can severely affect industries that are tightly related to global marketplaces or supply chains.

By remaining updated on industry trends and disruptions, you may anticipate future skill requirements, uncover emerging opportunities, and position yourself as a valued asset in your chosen sector.

Industry-Specific Challenges:
Each industry faces its own unique set of problems that experts must handle. Understanding these problems will help you make informed career decisions and establish ways to overcome potential obstacles. Some frequent industry-specific difficulties may include:

1. Competition and market saturation: Highly competitive industries, such as banking, media, or entertainment, may encounter issues linked to market saturation, making it difficult for newcomers to get entry-level positions or gain a footing in the industry.

2. Rapidly changing technologies: Industries like information technology, engineering, or healthcare typically battle with the need to continuously adapt to new and emerging technologies, requiring ongoing professional development and upskilling.

3. Regulatory compliance and ethical issues: Highly regulated industries, such as finance, healthcare, or legal services, must manage complex compliance standards, ethical considerations, and potential legal implications.

4. Diversity and inclusion difficulties: Some industries may have challenges relating to diversity, equity, and inclusion, such as gender or racial imbalances, unconscious prejudices, or lack of representation in leadership roles.

5. Work-life balance and burnout: Certain fields, including consulting, law, or investment banking, are recognized for rigorous work schedules and high-stress conditions, which can contribute to difficulty in maintaining work-life balance and preventing burnout.

By establishing an awareness of these industry-specific problems, you may better prepare yourself to manage potential obstacles, build coping techniques, and foster the resilience and adaptability necessary for long-term success in your chosen area.

Strategies for Gaining Industry Insights:

To get a greater awareness of industry-specific difficulties and complexities, explore the following strategies:

1. Informational interviews: Conduct informational interviews with professionals in your preferred sector to acquire first-hand insights into their experiences, issues, and opinions.

2. **Industry research**: Utilize industry periodicals, trade journals, internet forums, and professional associations to stay informed about trends, issues, and best practices within your sector.

3. **Mentorship and work shadowing**: Seek mentorship opportunities or job shadowing experiences with experienced professionals who can provide assistance and share their industry knowledge and skills.

4. **Professional development events**: Attend industry conferences, seminars, or workshops to learn from subject matter experts, network with professionals, and remain up-to-date on emerging trends and advancements.

5. **Case studies and scenario analysis**: Engage in case study analysis or scenario-based learning exercises to enhance critical thinking and problem-solving abilities in the context of industry-specific difficulties and situations.

By actively searching out industry-specific knowledge and insights, you may better prepare yourself for the realities and challenges of your desired area, establish a competitive edge, and position yourself for long-term success in navigating the subtleties and dynamics of your chosen career path.

Chapter Seven

Mastering the Job Search and Recruitment Process

Developing Effective Job Search Strategies and Resources

Navigating the job search process may be both exciting and challenging, but having a well-planned approach and employing the correct tools can dramatically boost your chances of success. Whether you're a new graduate or a seasoned professional, successfully managing your job search is vital for getting your desired post and furthering your career.

Job Search Strategies:

1. **Define your goals**: Clearly explain your desired job title, industry, geographical preferences, and non-negotiable criteria. This clarity will help you focus your search efforts and avoid exploring opportunities that don't correspond with your aims.

2. **Build a tailored resume and cover letter**: Tailor your resume and cover letter to each employment opportunity, showcasing your relevant abilities, experiences, and accomplishments that directly meet the job requirements.

3. **Leverage your network**: Inform your personal and professional network about your job hunt, and ask for referrals, introductions, or advice. Networking can often reveal unadvertised career opportunities and provide you with a competitive advantage.

4. **Utilize job search tools**: Take advantage of numerous job search resources, including online job boards, company websites, professional

associations, career fairs, and your university's career services center.

5. Optimize your online presence: Ensure that your professional internet presence (e.g., LinkedIn profile, personal website) is up-to-date, polished, and consistent with your career goals. Employers routinely study candidates online.

6. Stay organized: Develop a method to manage your job applications, follow-ups, and communication with possible employers. This will help you remain on top of your job search activities and ensure quick responses.

Job Search Resources:

1. Online job boards: Sites like Indeed, LinkedIn, and industry-specific job boards can be helpful sources for locating job ads and uploading your resume for potential employers to find.

2. **Company websites**: Many organizations offer job openings directly on their websites, typically before listing on job boards. Regularly check the career sections of companies you're interested in.

3. **Professional associations**: Industry-specific professional associations generally feature job boards, career information, and networking events that can link you with possible employers and job possibilities.

4. **University career services**: Your college or university's career services center can provide vital tools, including job advertisements, resume evaluations, practice interviews, and career counseling.

5. **Networking events**: Attend industry events, conferences, or meetings to connect with professionals in your target field and hear about prospective job openings or impending possibilities.

6. Recruiters and staffing companies: Consider dealing with reputed recruiters or staffing organizations that specialize in your sector or job function. They can help connect you with potential employers and work prospects.

Optimizing Your Job Search:

1. **Customize your approach:** Tailor your job search strategy and materials for each opportunity, highlighting your most relevant talents and experiences.

2. **Stay persistent and organized:** The job search process can be time-consuming and tough, so it's crucial to stay organized, motivated, and persistent in your efforts.

3. **Seek feedback:** Ask trustworthy professionals, mentors, or career advisers to examine your job search materials and provide feedback on areas for improvement.

4. Continuously study and upskill: Identify gaps in your knowledge or skills and aggressively pursue professional development opportunities to boost your marketability.

5. Maintain a good attitude: Approach the job search process with a positive perspective, resilience, and a willingness to learn from each experience, whether successful or not.

By adopting successful job search methods, leveraging the relevant resources, and improving your approach, you may boost your chances of standing out to potential employers and landing your desired job opportunity.

Acing Interviews and Negotiating Job Offers

Interviews are a vital component of the job search process, as they provide an opportunity for employers to examine your qualifications, skills, and fit for the role. Excelling in interviews demands rigorous preparation, great communication, and the ability to present your distinct value offer. Additionally, after you obtain a job offer, it's crucial to learn the art of negotiation to secure the finest possible terms and salary package.

Interview Preparation:

1. Research the company and role: Gather information on the company's mission, values, products or services, and industry trends. Understand the work criteria and responsibilities to personalize your responses properly.

2. Practice typical interview questions: Anticipate and practice answering common interview questions, such as "Tell me about yourself," "Why are you interested in this role?" and "What are your strengths and weaknesses?"

3. Prepare questions for the interviewer: Come prepared with intelligent questions that indicate your interest in the company and career, as well as your ability to think critically and engage in meaningful discourse.

4. Conduct mock interviews: Practice your interview skills with friends, family members, or career advisers to gain feedback on your body language, tone, and overall presentation.

5. Prepare relevant examples and accomplishments: Identify particular instances from your past experiences that illustrate your relevant abilities, successes, and ability to offer value to the role.

During the Interview:
1. Make a positive first impression: Dress professionally, come on time, and greet the

interviewer with a firm handshake and a confident manner.

2. Listen actively and answer thoroughly: Pay close attention to the interviewer's questions, and provide well-structured, intelligent responses that directly address the question being addressed.

3. Showcase your unique value proposition: Highlight your relevant talents, experiences, and accomplishments that indicate your fit for the role and the value you can offer to the organization.

4. Ask insightful questions: Engage in a dialogue by asking intelligent questions that indicate your interest and grasp of the organization and role.

5. Express enthusiasm and gratitude: Convey your real interest and enthusiasm for the opportunity, and thank the interviewer for their time and thoughtfulness.

Negotiating Job Offers:

1. Understand your worth: Research industry norms and compensation ranges for the role and region to ensure you have a realistic grasp of your market value.

2. Consider the full compensation package: While income is crucial, consider evaluating benefits, bonuses, equity, professional development opportunities, and work-life balance when assessing a job offer.

3. Negotiate strategically: If you receive an offer that doesn't match your expectations, gently negotiate certain parts of the offer, such as compensation, vacation days, or professional development possibilities.

4. Justify: Be prepared to explain why you believe your talents, experiences, and accomplishments justify a larger remuneration package or additional perks.

5. Know when to walk away: If the employer is unwilling to bargain or fulfill your realistic expectations, be prepared to respectfully decline the offer if it doesn't correspond with your goals and values.

Effective interview preparation and negotiation abilities are vital for gaining the greatest potential employment opportunity and remuneration package. By demonstrating your unique value offer, engaging in thoughtful dialogue, and negotiating strategically, you may position yourself for long-term career success and enjoyment.

Understanding Employee Rights, Benefits, and Compensation Packages

As you navigate the job search and recruitment process, it's crucial to understand your rights as an employee, as well as the many components of compensation packages and benefits offered by employers. Knowledge in these areas can empower you to make informed decisions, negotiate successfully, and safeguard your interests throughout your career journey.

Employee Rights:

1. Equal Employment Opportunity (EEO): Federal and state laws ban employment discrimination based on race, color, religion, sex (including pregnancy, gender identity, and sexual orientation), national origin, age, disability, or genetic information.

2. Fair Labor Rules Act (FLSA): This law regulates minimum wage, overtime compensation, recordkeeping, and child labor rules impacting full-time and part-time workers in the private sector and in federal, state, and municipal governments.

3. Family and Medical Leave Act (FMLA): FMLA permits eligible employees of covered employers to take unpaid, job-protected leave for specific family and medical reasons with continuation of group health insurance coverage.

4. Occupational Safety and Health Administration (OSHA): OSHA creates and enforces regulations to promote safe and healthful working conditions by providing training, outreach, education, and assistance to companies and employees.

5. Worker's Compensation: This program provides compensation and medical benefits to employees who suffer job-related injuries or illnesses, regardless of fault.

6. Whistleblower Protection: Laws protect employees who disclose violations of federal law or regulations against reprisal, harassment, or adverse employment choices by their company.

Understanding your rights as an employee can help you recognize and handle any issues, such as discrimination, unfair labor practices, or workplace safety concerns. It's crucial to be aware of these rights and the resources available to protect your interests.

Compensation Packages:
1. Base salary: This is the fixed amount of money that an employer pays an employee for their labor, generally represented as an annual or hourly rate.

2. Bonuses and incentives: Many organizations give performance-based bonuses, sales commissions, or other incentives related to specific goals or achievements.

3. Equity compensation: Some companies, particularly startups or technology enterprises, may offer equity in the form of stock options, restricted stock units (RSUs), or employee stock ownership plans (ESOPs).

4. Retirement benefits: Employers may offer retirement savings programs, such as 401(k) plans, with or without employer matching payments.

5. Health insurance: Most businesses provide health insurance plans, which may include medical, dental, and vision care, with variable levels of premiums and deductibles.

6. Paid time off: This comprises vacation days, sick leave, personal days, and holidays, which might vary greatly among workplaces.

7. **Additional benefits**: Employers may offer extra advantages, such as tuition reimbursement, professional development opportunities, gym memberships, or employee assistance programs.

When considering job offers or negotiating compensation packages, it's crucial to analyze the full package, not just the base wage. A full grasp of these components can help you make informed decisions that correspond with your financial goals and aspirations.

Negotiating Compensation and Benefits:
1. Research industry standards: Gather data on average wage ranges and benefits packages for your chosen career, industry, and geographic area.

2. **Highlight your value proposition**: Be prepared to define your unique abilities, experiences, and accomplishments that support a larger remuneration package.

3. Prioritize your needs: Identify which components of the pay package are most essential to you (e.g., salary, equity, retirement benefits, vacation time) and target your talks accordingly.

4. Consider timing and negotiating strategy: Understand the appropriate time to negotiate (e.g., after receiving an offer) and approach the negotiation process with professionalism and diplomacy.

5. Be prepared to compromise: Recognize that negotiating often entails give-and-take, and be willing to compromise on certain elements while remaining firm on your priorities.

By understanding your rights as an employee, the components of compensation packages, and effective negotiation methods, you can advocate for yourself, achieve a fair and competitive offer, and put yourself up for long-term career success and financial stability.

Chapter Eight

Entrepreneurship and Self-Employment Considerations

Evaluating the Entrepreneurial Mindset and Opportunities

Entrepreneurship and self-employment offer exciting opportunities for individuals who possess a unique combination of talents, enthusiasm, and a willingness to embrace risk and uncertainty. However, before going on this route, it's necessary to examine your entrepreneurial attitude and identify suitable company prospects that correspond with your interests, abilities, and market demand.

The Entrepreneurial Mindset:

Successful entrepreneurs have certain characteristics and mindsets that help them overcome the obstacles and uncertainties of beginning and expanding a firm. These traits include:

1. **Passion and Perseverance**: Entrepreneurs are driven by a deep passion for their ideas and an unrelenting perseverance to overcome hurdles and disappointments.
2. **Risk Tolerance**: Entrepreneurship inevitably requires taking calculated risks, and successful entrepreneurs possess the capacity to analyze and manage risks successfully.
3. **Adaptability and Resilience**: The business landscape is ever-changing, and entrepreneurs must be adaptive and robust, ready to pivot and alter their strategy as needed.
4. **Creative Problem-Solving**: Entrepreneurs encounter a steady stream of obstacles, and their ability to think creatively and generate unique solutions is vital.

5. Self-Motivation and Discipline: As a self-employed individual, you must be self-motivated and disciplined, capable of setting objectives, managing time, and keeping focused without external scrutiny.

Assessing your compatibility with the entrepreneurial mindset is key. Consider completing personality evaluations, receiving feedback from mentors or professionals, and honestly examining your strengths, shortcomings, and appetite for risk.

Identifying Business Opportunities:
Identifying feasible company possibilities is the first stage in the entrepreneurial journey. Here are some techniques to help you find possible opportunities:

1. Solve a Problem: Look for unmet needs or difficulties in your community, industry, or personal life that you can address with a product or service.

2. Leverage Your Expertise: Capitalize on your unique abilities, knowledge, or experiences by delivering consulting, coaching, or specialized services.

3. Explore Emerging Trends: Stay updated about emerging trends, technology, or consumer habits that could provide new market opportunities.

4. Improve Existing Products or Services: Identify ways to improve upon existing products or services by providing innovative features, greater quality, or more efficient processes.

5. Franchising or Licensing: Consider franchising opportunities or licensing existing successful business models as a more formal road to entrepreneurship.

Conducting market research is vital to validate the viability of your business idea. Analyze the target market, competition, possible demand, and any regulatory or legal factors that may affect your venture.

Developing a Business Plan, Securing Funding, and Legal Requirements

Once you've found a feasible company possibility, the next stage is to construct a complete business plan and get the required finance to bring your idea to life. Additionally, understanding the legal requirements and compliance obligations is vital to guaranteeing the long-term success and sustainability of your enterprise.

Developing a Business Plan:
A well-crafted business plan acts as a blueprint for your entrepreneurial journey, directing your decision-making and helping you express your idea to potential investors, partners, or stakeholders. A typical business plan should include:

1. Executive Summary: A succinct outline of your business idea, market potential, and major objectives.

2. Company Overview: A full description of your business concept, including your products or services, target market, and competitive advantages.

3. Market Analysis: An in-depth analysis of your industry, target market, competition, and prospective market trends or obstacles.

4. Operations Plan: A complete explanation of your business operations, including logistics, supply chain management, and manufacturing or service delivery processes.

5. Management and Organization: An overview of your management team, organizational structure, and essential roles and duties.

6. Marketing and Sales Strategy: A thorough plan for promoting and selling your products or services, including price, distribution routes, and promotional tactics.

7. Financial Projections: Detailed financial predictions, including projected income statements, balance sheets, cash flow statements, and break-even analysis.

Securing Funding:

Launching and growing a successful business often requires access to finance. Explore the following funding possibilities and their relative benefits and cons:

1. Personal Savings and Assets: Using your resources might provide greater control and ownership, but it also entails significant financial risk.

2. Friends and Family: Seeking investments from friends and family might be a realistic alternative, but it's crucial to retain professionalism and control expectations.

3. Angel Investors: Angel investors are people or groups who donate financing to early-stage firms in exchange for stock ownership.

4. **Venture Capital**: Venture capitalists are professional investment firms that provide finance to high-growth startups, often in exchange for a considerable stock stake.

5. **Small Business Loans**: Various government-backed and private lending schemes are available to help entrepreneurs get capital for their firms.

6. **Crowdfunding**: Online crowdfunding platforms allow entrepreneurs to raise capital from a huge pool of individual investors or backers.

When soliciting finance, be prepared to offer a compelling business plan, demonstrate a strong understanding of your market and financials, and successfully articulate your vision and growth potential.

Legal Requirements and Compliance:
Navigating the legal landscape is critical for entrepreneurs to maintain compliance and reduce potential risks. Some major legal factors include:

1. **firm form (e.g., sole proprietorship, partnership, corporation):** Choose the right legal form for your firm depending on issues such as liability, taxation, and ownership.

2. **Licenses and Permits**: Obtain the essential licenses and permits required for your unique business type and location.

3. **Intellectual Property Protection**: Protect your ideas, inventions, and brands by gaining trademarks, patents, or copyrights as applicable.

4. **Employment Laws and rules**: Understand and comply with labor laws, worker's compensation standards, and employment rules.

5. **Tax duties**: Stay informed on federal, state, and local tax requirements, including income tax, sales tax, and payroll tax duties.

6. **Contracts and Agreements**: Ensure that contracts, agreements, and conditions of service are legally binding and safeguard your business interests.

Consulting with legal specialists, such as attorneys or accountants, can help you manage the complexity of legal compliance and ensure that your firm runs within the bounds of the law.

Balancing Risks and Rewards of Self-Employment

Entrepreneurship and self-employment offer the potential for considerable rewards, such as financial independence, the capacity to pursue your passions, and the flexibility to define your path. However, these rewards typically come with a distinct set of risks and challenges that must be properly assessed and managed.

Risks of Self-Employment:
1. **Financial Instability**: As an entrepreneur, your income may fluctuate, and you may endure

moments of financial insecurity, especially in the early phases of your business.

2. Lack of Benefits and Safety Net: Self-employed individuals often do not have access to traditional job benefits, such as health insurance, paid time off, or retirement plans.

3. Personal Liability: Depending on your business structure, you may be personally accountable for debts, legal troubles, or financial losses related to your organization.

4. Work-Life Balance Challenges: Entrepreneurship frequently entails long hours, blurring boundaries between work and personal life, and the constant need to manage many tasks.

5. Stress and Burnout: The responsibilities of managing all parts of a business, from operations to marketing to finances, can contribute to heightened stress levels and probable burnout.

Mitigating Risks:

While the hazards of self-employment are inherent, there are tactics you may adopt to mitigate and manage these issues effectively:

1. **Financial Planning and Management**: Develop a thorough financial plan that accounts for probable swings in income, unforeseen expenses, and long-term savings goals. Implement appropriate financial management methods, such as budgeting, cash flow management, and separating personal and business finances.

2. **Building a Support System**: Surround yourself with a solid support network, including mentors, advisers, and professionals who can provide guidance, accountability, and emotional support during your entrepreneurial journey.

3. **Continued Professional Development**: Continuously invest in learning new abilities, remaining up-to-date with industry trends, and

increasing your knowledge base to stay competitive and flexible in a continuously shifting market.

4. Work-Life Integration: Establish clear boundaries between work and personal life, and prioritize self-care activities that improve physical and mental well-being. Leverage productivity tools and tactics to optimize your time and energy.

5. Risk Management methods: Implement risk management methods such as acquiring proper insurance coverage, diversifying your revenue streams, and making contingency plans for unexpected setbacks or emergencies.

Rewards of Self-Employment:
Despite the hazards, entrepreneurship, and self-employment offer various potential rewards and benefits:

1. Financial Independence and Wealth Building: As a business owner, you can attain financial independence and develop long-term wealth via the growth and success of your endeavor.

2. Autonomy and Flexibility: Self-employment allows you to be your boss, create your schedule, and have better control over your work-life balance.

3. Personal and Professional Growth: Entrepreneurship provides an opportunity for ongoing learning, personal development, and the satisfaction of converting your hobbies into a successful firm.

4. Creating a Legacy: Building a successful business can generate a lasting legacy and potentially provide employment chances for others in your community.

5. Sense of Achievement and Fulfillment: The ability to pursue your passions, solve problems, and make a real difference through your entrepreneurial activities can lead to a deep sense of achievement and personal fulfillment.

Embracing an entrepreneurial attitude and pursuing self-employment needs a fine mix of risk-taking and risk management. By carefully evaluating the risks and rewards, building a sound business plan, acquiring suitable capital, and executing effective risk mitigation methods, you may position yourself for long-term success and personal fulfillment as an entrepreneur.

Chapter Nine

Strategies for Career Advancement and Transitions

Continuous Learning, Professional Development, and Upskilling

In today's continuously shifting employment market, continual learning, professional development, and upskilling have become crucial tactics for career advancement and long-term success. As industries and work responsibilities grow, remaining current with new information, skills, and technology is vital for maintaining a competitive edge and adjusting to shifting needs.

The Importance of Continuous Learning:

1. **Staying Relevant**: Industries and employment responsibilities are constantly impacted by technological breakthroughs, altering market trends, and developing client expectations. Continuous learning ensures that your skills and expertise stay relevant and valuable to companies.

2. **Career Advancement**: Acquiring new skills and expertise can open doors to new possibilities, promotions, and higher-level positions within your organization or industry.

3. **Adaptability**: The ability to learn and change quickly is a highly valued attribute in the modern job. Continuous learning creates adaptability, enabling you to pivot and embrace new challenges or responsibilities as needed.

4. **Personal Growth**: Learning is a lifelong process that adds to personal growth, intellectual stimulation, and a sense of accomplishment and joy.

5. Competitive Advantage: Continuous learners have a significant advantage in the job market, as they can demonstrate a dedication to self-improvement and a determination to keep ahead of industry trends.

Professional Development Strategies:

1. Formal Education: Consider obtaining additional degrees, certificates, or specialized training programs to boost your competence and reputation in your field.

2. Online Learning: Leverage online educational resources, such as massive open online courses (MOOCs), webinars, and online tutorials, to learn new skills and knowledge at your own pace and convenience.

3. Conferences and Seminars: Attend industry conferences, workshops, and seminars to remain up-to-date with the latest trends, best practices, and emerging technology in your sector.

4. Professional Associations: Join relevant professional associations or organizations, which typically offer educational resources, networking opportunities, and access to industry experts and mentors.

5. On-the-Job Training: Seek out possibilities for on-the-job training, job shadowing, or stretch assignments inside your present business to improve your abilities and acquire exposure to new areas.

6. Mentorship & Coaching: Engage with seasoned professionals or industry experts who can provide direction, share their knowledge and ideas, and help your career advancement.

Upskilling:

Upskilling refers to the process of gaining new skills or strengthening current ones to suit the growing demands of the labor market or a specific role. Some major areas for upskilling may include:

1. **Technical Skills**: Developing skills in new technologies, programming languages, software applications, or digital tools relevant to your industry or intended career.

2. **Soft Skills**: Enhancing interpersonal skills such as communication, leadership, emotional intelligence, teamwork, and problem-solving, which are highly valued across numerous industries.

3. **Industry-related Knowledge**: Gaining in-depth knowledge and experience in emerging trends, legislation, or best practices related to your industry or sector.

4. **Cross-Functional Skills**: Acquiring skills and information from complementary subjects or

disciplines that can extend your viewpoints and boost your worth inside your business or industry.

By embracing a philosophy of continuous learning, actively pursuing professional development opportunities, and proactively upskilling, you may position yourself for ongoing career progress, increased job stability, and the capacity to negotiate the ever-changing terrain of the modern workforce.

Seeking Mentors, Sponsors, and Building Professional Networks

Building and cultivating solid professional relationships is a vital component of career progress and success. Seeking out mentors, finding sponsors, and actively establishing a healthy professional network can provide crucial support, guidance, and opportunities along your career journey.

The Power of Mentorship:

A mentor is an experienced and trusted advisor who provides guidance, shares knowledge, and offers support and encouragement to assist you navigate your career path. Effective mentorship relationships can give several benefits, including:

1. Career Guidance: Mentors can give insights, guidance, and viewpoints based on their own experiences, helping you make educated decisions about your career objectives and methods.

2. Skill Development: Mentors can discover areas for professional improvement, provide comments on your strengths and limitations, and recommend techniques for skill development.

3. Networking prospects: Mentors can introduce you to their professional networks, opening doors to new connections, employment prospects, or industry insights.

4. Motivation and Encouragement: Mentors can provide motivation, encouragement, and a supportive sounding board during tough times or moments of uncertainty.

5. Access to Industry Knowledge: Mentors with substantial industry expertise can give essential insights, best practices, and insider knowledge that will help you traverse your chosen sector more efficiently.

Finding and Building Sponsorship:
In addition to mentors, having important sponsors within your business or sector can be a significant accelerator for professional progress. Sponsors are senior-level professionals who actively advocate for your professional advancement and showcase your successes and potential to key decision-makers.

Building sponsorship partnerships involves:

1. **Identifying Potential Sponsors**: Look for senior leaders or influencers within your business or sector who have a track record of supporting and advocating for rising talent.

2. **Demonstrating Your Value**: Consistently perform high-quality work, take on challenging assignments, and actively contribute to the success of your team or business.

3. **Building Visibility**: Seek out opportunities to exhibit your talents, accomplishments, and leadership potential to potential sponsors.

4. **Fostering Relationships**: Cultivate genuine relationships with potential sponsors by seeking their assistance, sharing your career ambitions, and showing thanks for their support.

5. **Reciprocating Support**: Be willing to provide your time, skills, and assistance to your sponsors

when appropriate, building a mutually beneficial relationship.

Expanding Your Professional Network:
A powerful professional network can provide access to significant employment prospects, market insights, and possible mentors or sponsors. Building and maintaining a strong network involves:

1. **Attending Industry Events**: Participate in conferences, seminars, networking events, or professional association meetings to connect with others in your sector or adjacent industries.

2. **Leveraging Social Media**: Utilize platforms like LinkedIn, Twitter, or industry-specific online forums to interact with professionals, share content, and engage in debates.

3. **Informational Interviews**: Conduct informational interviews with individuals in your

target field or industry to learn about their jobs, and career pathways, and acquire insights into future opportunities.

4. Alumni Networks: Engage with your university or college alumni networks, which can provide useful connections and potential employment leads or mentorship opportunities.

5. Providing Value: Offer assistance, offer expertise, or provide referrals to individuals in your network, building a reciprocal relationship of mutual support and value exchange.

6. Following Up and Maintaining Connections: Regularly follow up with your network, offer updates on your professional achievements, and stay involved to cultivate and grow these ties over time.

By actively seeking out mentors, creating sponsorship relationships, and cultivating a strong professional network, you can benefit from valuable counsel, support, and access to opportunities that can push your career progress and advancement.

Navigating Career Pivots, Transitions, and Alternative Pathways

In today's dynamic employment market, career trajectories are often non-linear, and individuals may need to manage multiple pivots, transitions, or alternate tracks during their professional journey. Embracing flexibility, adaptability, and a readiness to explore new options can open doors to personal growth, fulfillment, and long-term work success.

Understanding Career Transitions:
Career transitions can occur for several reasons, including personal growth, shifting interests, industry transformations, or external influences

such as economic conditions or technology disruptions. Common types of career transitions include:

1. **Job Changes**: Moving from one role or organization to another within the same industry or area.

2. **Industry Shifts**: Transitioning to a new industry or sector, typically using transferable talents and experiences.

3. **Entrepreneurial Ventures**: Pursuing self-employment or beginning a new business endeavor.

4. **Career Reinvention**: Completely altering career pathways or fields, involving major upskilling or retraining.

5. **Semi-Retirement or Encore Careers**: Transitioning into alternative employment arrangements, such as consulting, teaching, or pursuing passion projects later in one's career.

Navigating job transitions effectively takes self-reflection, strategic preparation, and a willingness to welcome change and personal growth.

Exploring Alternative Career Pathways:
In addition to standard career trajectories, individuals may opt to pursue alternative courses that correspond with their values, interests, and lifestyle preferences. Some alternate job opportunities include:

1. Freelancing or Consulting: Working as an independent contractor or consultant, providing specialized services to many clients or organizations.

2. Portfolio Careers: Combining many part-time or project-based roles across various industries or disciplines, creating a broad and flexible work experience.

3. Remote or Location-Independent Work: Leveraging technology to work remotely or from anywhere in the world, giving greater flexibility and work-life balance.

4. Social Entrepreneurship: Pursuing entrepreneurial enterprises that prioritize social or environmental impact alongside financial goals.

5. Passion enterprises or Creative Pursuits: Dedicating time and resources to personal passions, artistic activities, or creative enterprises that may or may not yield cash.

Exploring different professional options can provide greater liberty, work-life balance, and the possibility to pursue various hobbies or passions simultaneously.

Strategies for Navigating Career Transitions and Pivots:

1. Self-Assessment and Reflection: Conduct a thorough self-assessment of your beliefs, interests, talents, and career aspirations to find viable paths that correspond with your goals and priorities.

2. Research and Exploration: Gather knowledge about potential career pathways, industries, or alternative employment arrangements through informational interviews, job shadowing, or online research.

3. Skill Development and Upskilling: Identify and acquire any relevant skills, certifications, or education required for your intended transition or pivot.

4. Networking and Relationship Building: Leverage your professional network, mentors, and industry connections to get insights, guidance, and potential opportunities relating to your career move.

5. Financial Planning: Assess your financial condition and design a strategy to manage any potential revenue fluctuations or expenses linked with your career transition.

6. Building a Transition Plan: Develop a complete transition plan that contains your goals, schedule, action stages, and contingency plans to manage your career pivot or shift effectively.

7. Embracing a Growth Mindset: Approach career transitions with an open mind, a desire to learn and adapt, and a focus on personal and professional growth.

Navigating professional pivots, changes, and alternative trajectories can be tough but also rewarding. By embracing flexibility, undertaking thorough self-assessment and research, building a strong support network, and developing a complete transition plan, you can uncover new chances for personal and professional fulfillment throughout your career journey.

Chapter Ten

Long-Term Career Planning and Financial Wellness

Aligning Short-Term and Long-Term Career Goals

Navigating a satisfying and successful profession involves a balance between short-term and long-term ambitions. While immediate objectives may focus on finding your first job or acquiring practical experience, it's crucial to maintain an eye on the wider picture and align your actions with your long-term aspirations.

Short-term career goals are often achievable within a few years and act as stepping stones towards more significant achievements. These may include gaining a certain degree or certification, acquiring appropriate work experience through internships or entry-level roles, or developing specialized talents that boost your marketability. Short-term goals provide a feeling of direction and motivation, helping you stay focused and make progress toward your ultimate aims.

However, it's vital to note that short-term goals should be matched with your long-term professional ambition. Long-term goals describe your desires over a longer extended period, often spanning five, ten, or even twenty years. These aspirations involve bigger desires, such as earning leadership roles, building competence in a certain profession, starting a business, or reaching financial independence.

To effectively match your short-term and long-term career goals, begin by completing a complete self-assessment. Reflect on your values, interests, strengths, and limitations. Identify the areas that excite and fulfill you, as well as those that may require further development or research. This self-awareness will serve as a basis for developing meaningful goals that resonate with your real self.

Next, visualize your ideal career path and the milestones you intend to attain along the route. Consider aspects such as your ideal work atmosphere, level of responsibility, earning potential, and work-life balance preferences. This long-term vision will help you in establishing short-term goals that move you in the right direction.

Break down your long-term ambitions into small, actionable stages. For instance, if your ultimate aim is to become a successful entrepreneur, your short-term goals may involve getting relevant industry expertise, producing a sound business plan, building a professional network, and securing capital.

Regularly assess and revise your goals when circumstances change or new possibilities arise. Life is dynamic, and your goals should be flexible enough to adjust to developing events. Maintain an open mindset and be willing to pivot as necessary, while still keeping your long-term vision in sight.

Seek for mentors and people in your desired field who can provide assistance and insights. Their experiences and recommendations can help you identify potential bottlenecks, alternate paths, and strategies for connecting your short-term actions with your long-term ambitions.

Remember, the route toward your long-term job goals is rarely a straight line. Embrace diversions, failures, and learning chances as valuable experiences that influence your growth and resilience. Celebrate minor triumphs along the way, since they act as stepping stones towards your ultimate objectives.

By linking your short-term and long-term work goals, you build a roadmap that guarantees your efforts are purposeful and linked with your real aspirations. This coherence boosts your focus, drive, and decision-making abilities, ultimately leading to a more full and rewarding career experience.

Work-Life Balance, Stress Management, and Personal Fulfillment

In the pursuit of professional success, it's easy to become overwhelmed by the demands of work, frequently at the sacrifice of personal well-being and contentment. However, maintaining a healthy balance between job objectives and home life is vital for general satisfaction, productivity, and long-term sustainability. Effective stress management and promoting personal fulfillment are essential components of this fragile balancing.

Work-life balance is a dynamic situation that requires continual examination and change. It entails distributing time and energy appropriately between professional tasks and personal hobbies, ensuring that neither aspect dominates or compromises the other. This balance looks different for everyone, as individuals have diverse priorities, lifestyles, and life stages.

To create a healthy work-life balance, start by identifying your basic values and priorities. What parts of life bring you the most joy, fulfillment, and feeling of purpose? For some, it may be spending quality time with family, pursuing hobbies or artistic interests, or engaging in physical and mental wellness activities. Once you have clarity on your priorities, you can make conscious choices about how to devote your time and energy properly.

Setting limits is key to preserving work-life balance. Establish clear parameters for when you will allocate time to work and when you will prioritize personal responsibilities. This may involve setting defined work hours, barring email or phone access during personal time, or creating designated locations for work and relaxation. Communicate these limits effectively with coworkers, managers, and loved ones to ensure they are respected.

Time management and organization skills are key advantages in establishing a work-life balance. Utilize tools and tactics, such as calendars, to-do lists, and productivity apps, to prioritize activities and manage your schedule successfully. Learn to delegate or say no to things that fall beyond your primary responsibilities or priorities, and don't hesitate to ask for support when needed.

Stress is an inevitable part of life, but it's vital to learn good coping techniques to minimize burnout and maintain general well-being. Identify your specific stress triggers and build personalized techniques to handle them. This may involve practicing mindfulness techniques, indulging in physical activity, seeking counseling or therapy, or simply taking regular breaks to recharge.

Personal fulfillment is tightly connected with work-life balance and stress management. When you prioritize activities and pursuits that correspond with your beliefs and add joy and meaning to your life, you build a sense of purpose and fulfillment that transcends professional achievements.

Nurture your relationships with loved ones, friends, and supporting communities. Strong social relationships not only provide emotional support but also contribute to a sense of belonging and fulfillment. Make time for shared experiences, great conversations, and important connections that enrich your life beyond work.

Engage in hobbies, artistic outlets, or recreational activities that allow you to explore your passions and express your individuality. These pursuits can serve as outlets for stress release, personal growth, and rejuvenation, ultimately increasing your general well-being and professional performance.

Continuous learning and self-development are vital components of personal fulfillment. Embrace opportunities for progress, whether through formal education, professional development courses, or self-directed learning. Expanding your knowledge and abilities not only boosts your professional possibilities but also generates a sense of accomplishment and intellectual stimulation.

Regularly examine and alter your work-life balance and personal fulfillment tactics. Life is dynamic, and your objectives and circumstances may change over time. Remain flexible and adaptive, and don't hesitate to seek advice from professionals, mentors, or loved ones when needed.

By actively pursuing work-life balance, effective stress management, and personal fulfillment, you develop a well-rounded existence that promotes your general well-being, productivity, and pleasure. This holistic approach not only boosts your career achievement but also enriches your path, leading to a more meaningful and satisfying life experience.

Financial Literacy, Retirement Planning, and Wealth-Building Strategies

Financial awareness and proactive planning are crucial components of long-term career success and personal well-being. Understanding core financial principles, planning retirement strategies, and adopting wealth-building approaches can give you a firm basis for financial security and independence throughout your life.

Financial literacy comprises a broad variety of information and abilities linked to personal finance, including budgeting, saving, investing, managing debt, and understanding taxation. Developing financial literacy from an early age empowers individuals with the tools to make informed decisions about their money, build healthy financial habits, and attain long-term financial goals.

Budgeting is a vital part of financial literacy. It entails analyzing income and costs, identifying areas of overspending, and allocating monies towards various financial goals, such as housing, transportation, food, entertainment, and savings. Budgeting tools, such as spreadsheets or mobile apps, can ease this process and provide vital insights into spending habits, helping you to make smart adjustments.

Saving is another key component of financial literacy. Establishing an emergency fund, equivalent to several months' worth of living expenses, can provide a safety net in case of unexpected circumstances or job loss. Additionally, setting aside funds for specific purposes, such as purchasing a home, supporting education, or starting a business, might help you attain your financial objectives more successfully.

Understanding debt management is equally vital. While some forms of debt, such as school loans or mortgages, may be important investments, it's essential to distinguish between good and bad debt. High-interest consumer debt, such as credit card balances, can quickly spiral out of control, leading to financial distress and harming credit ratings. Developing measures to remove high-interest debt and keeping a healthy credit score can open doors to improved lending opportunities and financial security.

Investing is a great instrument for developing long-term wealth and achieving financial freedom. While investing may seem frightening, gaining a fundamental understanding of investment instruments, such as stocks, bonds, mutual funds, and real estate, may demystify the process. Consulting with financial advisors, performing research, and starting with low-risk investments can help you progressively acquire confidence and grow your portfolio over time.

Retirement planning is a critical part of long-term financial well-being. Understand the various retirement accounts available, such as 401(k) plans, Individual Retirement Accounts (IRAs), and defined benefit plans, and their unique tax advantages. Start saving for retirement as early as possible, even with small amounts, to take advantage of compound interest and optimize your prospects for a happy retirement.

Wealth-building tactics extend beyond typical investing and retirement preparation. Entrepreneurship and passive income streams, such as rental properties, royalties, or online enterprises, can give extra sources of income and expedite wealth growth. However, it's crucial to thoroughly examine the risks and potential rewards of these endeavors and get professional assistance when necessary.

Another key part of financial literacy is understanding taxation and its impact on your total financial picture. Familiarize yourself with tax rules, deductions, and credits about your case, and explore techniques for minimizing tax responsibilities while keeping compliance with regulations.

Estate planning is an often overlooked but vital component of long-term financial planning. Develop a thorough estate plan that includes a will, trusts, and other legal instruments to guarantee your assets are dispersed according to your intentions and to prevent potential disagreements or legal issues for your beneficiaries.

Continuously educate yourself on financial matters through reading, attending seminars, or obtaining help from financial professionals. The financial landscape is continuously shifting, and staying updated about new rules, investment possibilities, and wealth-building tactics can help you adapt and make informed decisions.

Encourage financial knowledge throughout your family and social circles. Share your expertise and experiences, and create open discussions about money management, goal-setting, and long-term financial planning. Building a supportive group can bring accountability, incentives, and useful insights for achieving financial success.

Embracing financial literacy, retirement planning, and wealth-building methods from an early stage in your career can have a profound impact on your long-term financial well-being. By establishing a firm understanding of personal finance fundamentals, applying proactive planning, and cultivating healthy financial habits, you can gain greater financial stability, independence, and the capacity to pursue your life goals with confidence.

Exclusive Bonus

20 most Common Interview Questions & How to Answer Them

1. Tell me about yourself.
This is generally one of the first questions asked in an interview, and it's an opportunity to present a succinct and convincing review of your background, experiences, and qualifications. When answering this question, attempt to strike a balance between promoting your professional successes and offering important personal information that demonstrates your personality and values.

Sample Answer: "I'm a driven and passionate [your profession] with [number] years of experience in [relevant industry or field]. Throughout my career, I've had the opportunity to work on various projects that have honed my skills in [relevant skills or expertise]. What motivates me most is [your passion or driving force], and I thrive in collaborative environments where I can contribute my problem-solving abilities and innovative ideas. Outside of work, I'm an avid [hobby or interest] and actively participate in [community involvement or volunteer work]."

2. What are your biggest strengths?

This question allows you to showcase your most relevant abilities, talents, and traits that make you an outstanding fit for the role. When answering, focus on abilities that directly connect to the job criteria and provide specific instances to explain how you've implemented these strengths in previous employment.

Sample Answer: "One of my greatest strengths is [strength] which has been invaluable in my [profession or industry]. For example, in my previous role as [previous position], I successfully [specific accomplishment or example] by leveraging my [strength]. Additionally, I pride myself on my [another strength], which has allowed me to [another example or accomplishment]."

3. What are your major weaknesses?

While this question may sound difficult, it's an opportunity to display self-awareness and a commitment to personal progress. When answering, identify a genuine weakness, but emphasize on how you're actively striving to improve or lessen its impact.

Sample Answer: "One area I've been working on is [weakness]. In the past, this has been a challenge for me, especially when [specific example or situation]. However, I've taken steps to address this weakness by [strategies or actions you've taken to improve], and I've seen significant progress in [specific improvement or result]."

4. Why are you interested in this role/company?

Employers prefer to employ individuals who are interested in the role and have a strong understanding of the company's mission, values, and culture. In your answer, demonstrate your study and knowledge of the organization, and explain how your talents and experiences connect with the role and firm.

Sample Answer: "I'm excited about the opportunity to join [company name] because of [specific reasons, such as the company's mission, values, products/services, growth potential, or culture]. Additionally, this role aligns perfectly with my [relevant skills, experiences, or interests], and I believe my [specific qualifications or achievements] would be a valuable contribution to the team. I'm particularly drawn to [aspects of the company or role that excites you], and I'm eager to leverage my experience to [specific contribution or impact you hope to make]."

5. What are your career goals?

Employers want to hire people who are motivated and have a clear vision for their professional development. When answering this question, describe your long-term professional ambitions and how the current role fits into your broader plan.

Sample Answer: "In the long term, my goal is to [specific career goal or aspiration, such as a leadership role, subject matter expertise, or entrepreneurial venture]. This role as [current position] at [company name] aligns perfectly with my goal because it would allow me to [specific skills, experiences, or knowledge you hope to gain]. Additionally, I'm excited about the potential for growth within the company, and I'm eager to take on increasing responsibilities and challenges that will help me develop [relevant skills or competencies] in preparation for my [long-term goal]."

6. Why are you quitting your current job?

When answering this question, it's crucial to be professional and avoid speaking adversely about your present or prior company. Instead, focus on the positive reasons for seeking a new opportunity, such as career progression, better alignment with your beliefs or goals, or a desire for new challenges.

Sample Answer: "While I've gained valuable experience and appreciate the opportunities provided by my current employer, I'm at a point in my career where I'm ready for a new challenge that aligns more closely with my long-term goals. This role at [company name] offers the opportunity to [specific aspects of the new role that excite you, such as new responsibilities, professional growth, or alignment with your interests]. Additionally, I'm drawn to [company name]'s [specific aspects of the company's culture, mission, or values that resonate with you]."

7. How do you handle disagreement or stress in the workplace?

This question examines your ability to manage hard situations and maintain professionalism under pressure. When answering, share a particular example of how you've effectively managed disagreement or stress in the past, demonstrating your problem-solving skills and emotional intelligence.

Sample Answer: "In any workplace, conflicts and stressful situations are bound to arise. When faced with such challenges, my approach is to remain calm and objective, actively listen to all parties involved, and work collaboratively to find a mutually agreeable solution. For example, in my previous role, there was a disagreement between two team members over [specific conflict or situation]. To resolve the issue, I [specific actions you took to address the conflict or manage the stress], which ultimately led to [positive outcome or resolution]."

8. Describe a time when you encountered a huge hurdle and how you overcame it.

This question examines your problem-solving ability, resilience, and capacity for growth. When answering, find a specific and relevant example that displays your capacity to think critically, take initiative, and endure in the face of adversity.

Sample Answer: "One of the most significant challenges I've faced was [specific challenge or obstacle]. Initially, I [describe your initial reaction or approach], but when that didn't yield the desired results, I reassessed the situation and [specific actions you took to overcome the challenge]. Through this experience, I learned [valuable lessons or skills gained], which has made me [specific positive outcome or growth resulting from the experience]."

9. How do you prioritize and manage multiple activities or projects?

Employers want to recruit people who are organized, efficient, and able to manage their time and workload successfully. When answering, share specific examples of tactics or tools you use to prioritize assignments, fulfill deadlines, and ensure high-quality work.

Sample Answer: "Effective time management and prioritization are essential in my role as [current or previous role]. When faced with multiple tasks or projects, I begin by [specific strategy or tool you use, such as creating a to-do list, using a project management tool, or prioritizing based on deadlines or importance]. This allows me to [specific positive outcomes, such as meeting deadlines, delivering high-quality work, or managing stakeholder expectations]. For example, in my previous role, I was responsible for [specific example of managing multiple tasks or projects simultaneously], and by [specific actions or strategies used], I was able to [positive result or accomplishment]."

10. What motivates you in your work?

This question provides insight into your values, drivers, and what inspires you to achieve at your best. When answering, offer concrete examples of what inspires and energizes you in your work, whether it's a sense of accomplishment, learning new skills, contributing to a broader purpose, or working in a collaborative setting.

Sample Answer: "What motivates me most in my work is [specific motivator, such as a sense of accomplishment, learning opportunities, contributing to a larger purpose, or working collaboratively]. For example, in my previous role, I found it incredibly rewarding when [specific example of how your motivator inspired you or led to a positive outcome]. Working in an environment that [specific aspect of the work environment or company culture that aligns with your motivator] is important to me, as it allows me to [specific positive impact or contribution you aim to make]."

11. How would your coworkers describe you?

This question examines your self-awareness and provides insight into your interpersonal abilities and work style. When answering, offer concrete examples or feedback from colleagues that demonstrate your positive attributes, work ethic, and ability to interact effectively.

Sample Answer: "Based on feedback from previous colleagues, I believe they would describe me as [positive trait or characteristic, such as dedicated, collaborative, or adaptable]. For instance, one of my former managers commended me for [specific example or situation that demonstrates the trait]. Additionally, my colleagues have often remarked on my [another positive trait or characteristic] which has enabled me to [specific positive outcome or impact resulting from that trait]."

12. Describe a situation when you had to work in a team environment.

Employers reward applicants who can work well and contribute to a positive team atmosphere. When answering, describe a particular example of a successful team project or experience, highlighting your position, contributions, and how you managed any problems or disagreements within the team.

Sample Answer: "In my previous role, I was part of a cross-functional team tasked with [specific project or initiative]. As a team member, my responsibilities included [specific contributions or role within the team]. One of the challenges we faced was [specific challenge or conflict within the team], which I helped address by [specific actions or strategies used to resolve the issue]. Ultimately, our team was able to [have a positive outcome or accomplishment], which taught me the importance of [valuable lessons or skills gained from the experience]."

13. How do you stay current with industry trends and developments?

This question examines your dedication to continual learning and professional improvement. When answering, share specific examples of how you actively seek out and learn new knowledge and skills relevant to your sector or industry.

Sample Answer: "Staying current with industry trends and developments is essential in my field, as [specific reason or importance]. To ensure I'm up-to-date, I [specific actions or strategies you use, such as attending conferences or workshops, participating in professional associations, reading industry publications, or taking online courses]. For example, recently I [specific example of how you applied new knowledge or skills gained from professional development activities]."

14. What are your pay expectations?

This question allows the employer to determine if your expectations fit with the allocated salary range for the role. When answering, indicate a range based on your study into industry standards and the cost of living in the area, and express flexibility and a desire to negotiate.

Sample Answer: "Based on my research and experience in [relevant industry or field], my salary expectation for this role is in the range of [salary range]. However, I'm open to negotiation, and I'm primarily motivated by the opportunity to contribute my skills and expertise to [company name] and grow within the organization."

15. How do you handle constructive criticism or feedback?

Employers want to hire applicants who are open to feedback and motivated to ongoing improvement. When answering, share an example of how you've responded favorably to constructive criticism or comments in the past, emphasizing your development attitude and desire to learn and adapt.

Sample Answer: "I welcome constructive criticism and feedback as opportunities for personal and professional growth. In my previous role, my manager provided feedback that [specific area for improvement or feedback received]. Rather than becoming defensive, I [specific actions taken to address the feedback, such as seeking additional guidance, implementing new strategies, or taking a training course]. As a result, I was able to [positive outcome or improvement resulting from addressing the feedback]."

16. What are your strengths and shortcomings in a customer service role?

For customer-facing professions, employers want to assess your abilities to offer great service and manage problematic customer encounters. When answering, highlight relevant strengths that correspond with the role's needs, and address a true shortcoming while demonstrating how you're actively striving to improve.

Sample Answer: "One of my greatest strengths in a customer service role is [specific strength, such as patience, active listening, or problem-solving]. For example, in my previous role, I [specific example demonstrating strength in action]. However, an area I continue to work on is [specific weakness, such as assertiveness or handling difficult customers]. To address this, I've [specific actions taken to improve, such as taking a course or seeking feedback from mentors]."

17. How do you handle working under pressure or tight deadlines?

This question examines your ability to function well in high-stress situations and manage time well. When answering, describe a concrete example of a moment when you successfully met a tight deadline or worked under pressure, stressing the methods and talents you applied.

Sample Answer: "Working under pressure or tight deadlines is a common occurrence in my field, and I've developed strategies to manage stress and prioritize effectively. For example, in my previous role, I [specific situation or project with a tight deadline]. To ensure successful completion, I [specific actions taken, such as creating a detailed plan, delegating tasks, or working extended hours]. By [specific strategies or skills employed, such as time management or stress management techniques], I was able to deliver [positive outcome or result]."

18. What's your leadership style, and how do you motivate a team?

For professions that entail managing or leading others, employers want to understand your approach to leadership and capacity to inspire and motivate team members. When answering, discuss your leadership philosophy and include examples of how you've effectively encouraged and supported a team in the past.

Sample Answer: "My leadership style is [specific style, such as collaborative, visionary, or servant leadership], which involves [specific approach or behaviors, such as empowering team members, setting clear goals, or leading by example]. In my previous role in [leadership position], I motivated my team by [specific strategies used, such as recognizing achievements, providing growth opportunities, or fostering a positive work environment]. For example, [specific situation or example demonstrating your leadership style and ability to motivate the team]."

19. What are your long-term professional ambitions, and how does this role fit into them?

Employers seek to hire applicants who are devoted to their long-term professional development and consider the current work as a chance for progress. When answering, describe your long-term aims and how the role corresponds with your goals, stressing your passion and opportunity for progress within the firm.

Sample Answer: "My long-term career goal is to [specific long-term aspiration, such as reaching a leadership position, becoming a subject matter expert, or starting a business]. This role as [current position] at [company name] aligns perfectly with that goal because it will provide me with the opportunity to [specific skills, experiences, or knowledge you hope to gain]. I'm excited about the potential for growth and advancement within the company, and I'm eager to take on increasing responsibilities that will help me develop [relevant skills or competencies] in preparation for my [long-term goal]."

20. Do you have any queries for us?

Interviews are a two-way conversation, and employers expect candidates to come prepared with intelligent questions that indicate their enthusiasm and understanding of the role and organization.

When answering, have a few questions ready that highlight your curiosity, research, and eagerness to contribute to the organization's success.

Sample Questions:
- What are the major problems or opportunities facing the team/department currently?
- How would you describe the company's culture and values?
- What professional development opportunities are available for personnel in this role?
- Can you offer an example of a successful project or initiative that embodies the company's goal or values?
- What are the major performance criteria or goals for this role, and how is success measured?

By preparing thoughtful and targeted solutions to these frequent interview questions, you may effectively exhibit your qualifications, talents, and fit for the post, while demonstrating your professionalism, self-awareness, and enthusiasm for the opportunity.

www.ingramcontent.com/pod-product-compliance
Lightning Source LLC
Chambersburg PA
CBHW052154220526
45471CB00004B/1666